Computer Instruction Series

VOLUME 11

Microsoft® Office 2019 FOR KIDS

Making office applications fun!

WRITTEN BY SANDRA J. GAISER

G&M Consulting

COMPUTER INSTRUCTION SERIES, VOLUME 11

MICROSOFT OFFICE 2019 FOR KIDS

SANDRA J. GAISER

Illustrations by Nicholas Mortensen & Alyssa Mortensen where not otherwise credited

Liberty Hill, TX
Website: www.sgaiser.com • Email: sgaiser@gmail.com

Proudly printed in the United States of America

Published by G & M Consulting, August 2020

ISBN-13: 978-1-7352796-1-9

To Keith

I love you. Thank you for all your support.

To Nicholas & Alyssa

Thank you for all your help and advice. I love you both. ☺

To Mom & Dad

You always said I could do anything if I put my mind to it. I love & miss you guys.

To David Swarbrick

Thank you for the reason and the opportunity.

To all my One Day Academy students

Thank you for all the book-testing, editing tips & typo-locating!

Table of Contents

Lesson 1

1-Intro to Microsoft Office 2019 for Kids

There are a few things to know before we start using the applications.

Computers can be used for much more than email, shopping, connecting with your friends and games. People now use computers for almost everything: writing letters, making charts, making cards, news stories, sports information, music, and art. In fact, **it is difficult to name an industry that does not use computers daily**. You will also use computers daily in your schoolwork writing book reports, research papers, lab reports, etc. This book will teach you in a **fun way** to create all those things!

"App" is short for application

What is an application?

There are 3 general types of programs that computers run:

- BIOS
- Operating system
- Applications

The first is the BIOS: basic input/output system. This is built into the computer hardware and is also called **firmware**. It makes it possible for the computer to start up each time by controlling the keyboard, text display, hard drive and more without accessing any programs stored on a disk. This is the first program that runs when you start a computer.

The second type of program is the operating system. Operating systems help the applications and hardware talk to each other: keyboard to screen, word processor to printer. Examples of popular operating systems are Microsoft Windows®, Linux®, and Apple Lion®. The operating system is the second program that loads when you start a computer.

The third type of program is the application like we are going to use in class this year. These are programs written to perform a specific task like write a letter, add up numbers, make a greeting card, enhance photos or paint a picture. The applications load every time you open a new program. If you open too many applications at once, your computer can run very slowly or even freeze up.

Applications We Will Use

We will be using these Microsoft Office 2019 and Microsoft Windows 10 applications:

- Microsoft Word
- Microsoft Excel
- Microsoft PowerPoint
- Microsoft Publisher
- Microsoft Paint

Different Versions of Microsoft Office

The Step-By-Step directions in this book are for Microsoft Office version 2019. There aren't many differences between Microsoft Office versions 2016 and 2019, so if you have 2016, this book would be okay, but your specific instructions will be a little different.

> *If you have Office 2016, I recommend you get my book called Microsoft Office 2016for Kids. There are separate versions of this book for 2007 & 2010 users, too.*

The biggest difference is the **DRAW tab** in 2019 was added. Also added: A **Dictate** button and an **Editor** button. Notice the tab colors now match the ribbon instead of the title bar, and the username has a profile photo.

NEW Draw tab Microsoft Office 2019

NEW Dictate & Editor buttons

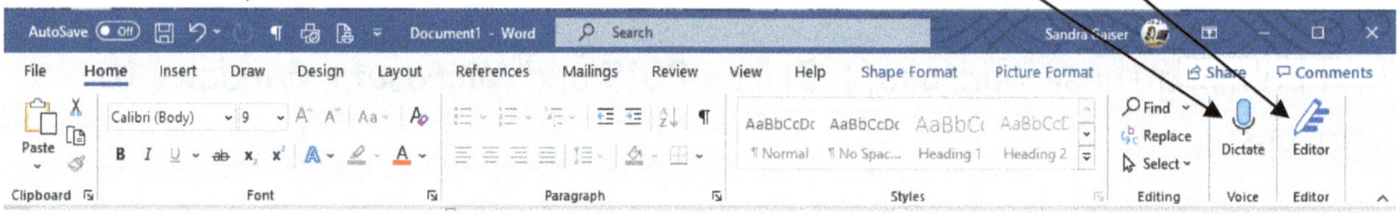

Ribbon tabs color matches title bar in Microsoft Office 2016

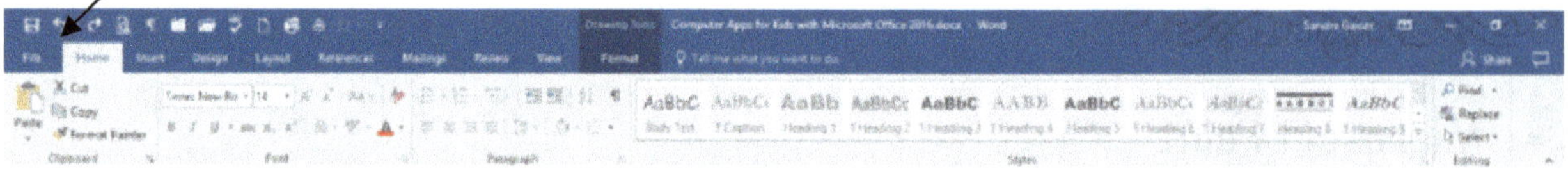

The Office 2019 Ribbon

The **Ribbon** is the command area at the top of the window in all Microsoft Office applications. It gives access to all the options available in each application for editing. Not all the options that are available are shown on the **Ribbon**. For those, you must use the **Dialog Box Launcher Button**. Above the **Ribbon** there is a small **Quick Access Toolbar**.

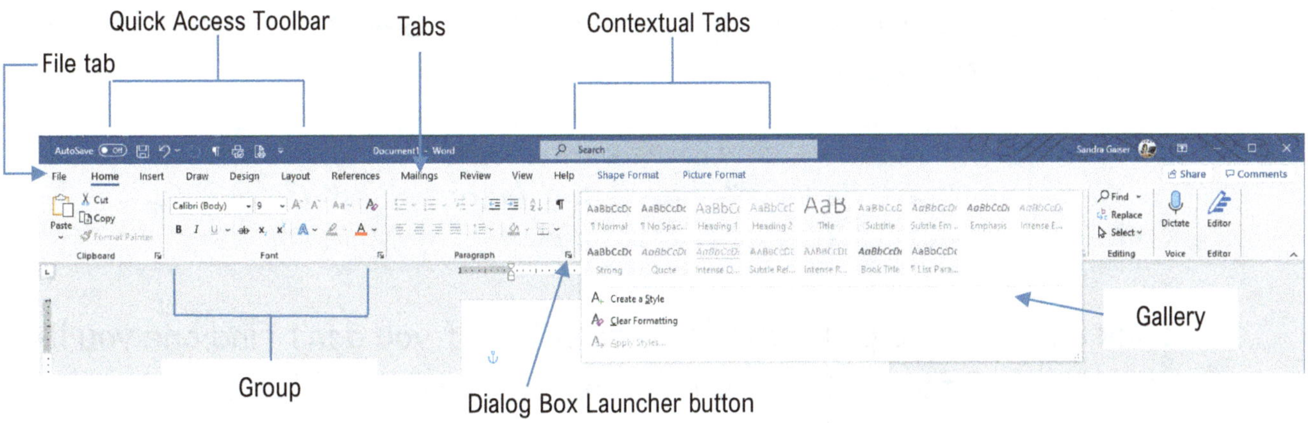

The Ribbon in Microsoft Word 2019

NOW IT'S YOUR TURN...

1. Open Microsoft Word either by searching for it or by clicking on it.
2. What version of Microsoft Office are you using today? __________

The **Ribbon** has **Tabs** across the top of it, like file folder tabs starting with the File tab.

NOW IT'S YOUR TURN...

Write down the names of all the tabs on the Ribbon in Microsoft Word:

_____ ______ _____ ______ ______ ________ _______ _______ ______

On each **Tab** are **buttons** that correspond to the name of the tab. For example, all the **View** options are on the **View tab** of the **Ribbon**. To change Tabs, simply click directly on the name of the Tab.

NOW IT'S YOUR TURN...

1. Click on the **Design Tab** on the **Ribbon**.
2. Click on **Page Color**.
3. Now hover your mouse ***slowly*** over each color. See it changing? This is called **Live Preview**

> *If your page color isn't changing as you hover the mouse over the colors, your "Live Preview" feature may be turned off. Go to File, Options, and check Enable Live Preview.*

4. Click on a color to pick your favorite color. If you don't find one you like, click **More Colors**. There are 2 tabs: Standard and Custom:

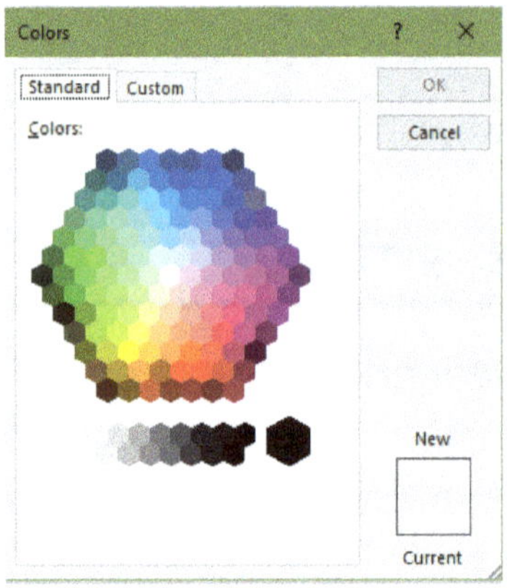

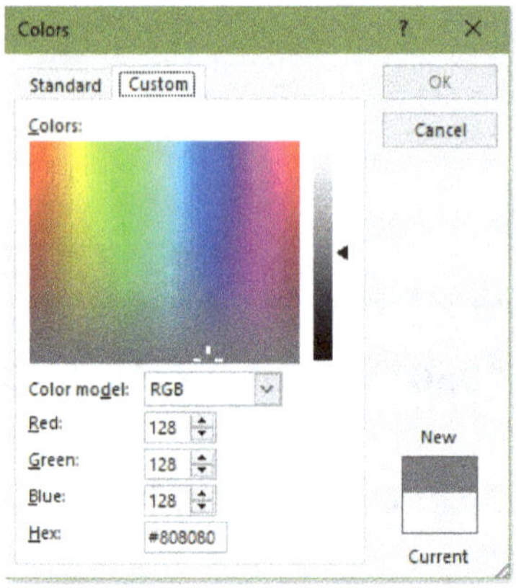

5. Now type your name. The font color will be white if you picked a dark color. It will be black it you picked a lighter color.
6. **QUESTION:** Will your page print this colorful way? **YES** or **NO** (Circle one)
7. Let's check: Click on the **File** tab.
8. Click on the word **Print** to see the **Print Preview**.
9. Why does it print this way? ______________________________

Contextual Tabs

These tabs pop up at the end of the **Ribbon** whenever you click on an item other than text, like a picture or a table. These **contextual tabs** contain specific buttons for that item that you clicked on like a Crop button for pictures on the Picture Tools contextual tab or the **Table Design Gallery** for a Table.

NOW IT'S YOUR TURN...

1. Click on the **Insert Tab** on the **Ribbon**
2. Click on **Pictures**
3. Click on **Online Pictures**
4. Select the **Apple** category and double-click on any apple picture to add it to your document.
5. Look at the end of the **Ribbon**. A new **Tab** was added, a **CONTEXTUAL TAB**.
6. Write down the name of the new tab here: ____________________

Groups

Items on the **Ribbon** are in **Groups**. Each **Group** is named at the bottom of the **Ribbon**. On the **Home tab** above, you can see the **Clipboard**, **Font**, **Paragraph**, and **Styles** groups. To the right of each **Group** name is a **Dialog Box Launcher**. It's a long name for the button that pops up an options window for the specific group.

NOW IT'S YOUR TURN...

1. Click on the **Home tab** on the **Ribbon**.
2. Write down the names of the **Groups** on the **Home Tab** of the **Ribbon** in Microsoft Word®:

________ ________ ________ ________ ________ ________ ________

Galleries

On the **Home tab** on the **Ribbon**, you can see the text **Styles Gallery**. As you hover your mouse over each one of these styles, you will see an **Auto Preview** of how that style would look if you clicked it to apply it.

NOW IT'S YOUR TURN...

---

1. Click on the **Home Tab** on the **Ribbon.**
2. Click inside the document page next to your name. Press **Enter**.
3. Type your full name.
4. Now hover your mouse ***slowly*** over each **Style** name in the **Style Gallery**. See it changing?
5. Click on Heading 1 and that **Style** will be applied to your name.

At Least 3 Ways to Do Everything and Sometimes 6!

One of the reasons computers are so confusing is that there are **at least 3 ways to do everything**. One person will show you one way, and another person will show you different way. Which is right? BOTH! The trick is to **find the way that works best for you and stick with it**. In this book, we will show you **one** way, but there are many others:

#1 - Left-click with mouse

First, as you probably know, you can always left-click with your mouse on something to accomplish some task, like clicking the **B** on the **Ribbon** to make text **BOLD**, for example.

But there's a 2nd way...

#2 - Right-click with mouse

The first way assumes you clicked with you **left** mouse button on something. Did you know there is a **right** mouse button? You can **right-click your mouse anywhere for a short menu** of only the options available right there. If you **right-click** on a word in a word processor, you can left-click on any of the choices that are shown, like the B for bold. This is really helpful since sometimes you don't even know what your choices are in a given area.

> **"When in doubt, right-click."**
> **--Yvette Schultz, Computer Trainer**

NOW IT'S YOUR TURN...

---

1. Hover the mouse over your first name that you typed.
2. **Right-click** your mouse.
3. What choices to you see? ________________________________

   ____
4. Click the **B** to bold your name.

Then, there's the 3rd way...

#3 – Keyboard shortcuts

Before the mouse was used to get around in computer programs, we either typed all commands or used **shortcut keystrokes**. Did you know that to bold text you can press **CTRL-B**?

NOW IT'S YOUR TURN...

---

1. Double-click your mouse to select your last name.
2. Hold down the CTRL key and tap the B key.
3. You last name should be BOLD now.

Cool, huh? There are a great number of keyboard shortcuts, and they are really handy, too. See the **Appendix** in the very back of this book for more **Keyboard Shortcuts**.

And then one more way....

#4 – Keyboard Access to Mouse Items

In addition to shortcut keystrokes, **there are alternate ways to use a computer** for people with disabilities or for people who prefer not to use a mouse. For example, in a word processor like Microsoft Word®, to access the commands on the **Ribbon** without a mouse, tap the **ALT** key. A bunch of boxes with numbers or letters will light up on the **Ribbon**. Simply press the key that corresponds with the command that you want.

NOW IT'S YOUR TURN...

---

1. Double-click your teacher's last name to select that whole word.
2. Tap **ALT**.
3. Press **H** for the **Home tab**, then **1** for the **Bold** button.

So, there 4 ways to bold a word! You pick which is right for you.

This book layout

It will help you to know how this book is laid out to help you learn quickly and easily. This way you can know what is coming up next and you will be prepared for it.

Table of Contents

This will tell you all the lessons in this book and what they go over. It will also help you find topics and projects when you are looking for them.

Lessons in this book

- Lesson 1: Introduction
- Lessons 2-34 we make projects

Each chapter has:

- A description of the project & What you will learn
- Step-by-step instructions to complete the project
- **Lesson Practice:** 1 day to practice what you have learned
- **Lesson Review:** A few questions to review what's in the chapter
- And, if needed, a **Planning for Our Next Lesson** section

Conventions in this book

When you see the folder icon, this means there is valuable information for you to read and learn. **Pay special attention here**.

When you see the big, gray keyboard, this indicates a **keyboard exercise** that you will practice in class when the instructor tells you to.

Ok, enough about this book, LET'S GET LEARNING!

Lesson Review:

1. What is an application?

   ____

2. Where is the **Ribbon** in Microsoft applications?

   ____

3. How many ways are there to do something on a computer?

   1 way 3 ways 6 ways

Planning for our next lesson:

1. **What kinds of stickers do you want to make to put on your computer notebook? (Animals, computers, food, etc.)**

   ____

2. **Which do you want to make (pick one):**

   ☐ A full page design

   ☐ Lots of smaller stickers to cut apart

Lesson

2

2-Making Stickers in Publisher

Stickers are easy with the right paper to print them on!

About Our Project

You can make a page of stickers in any of the Microsoft Office programs. We use Microsoft Publisher because you work on a "blank slate" with no margins or text wrapping to work against your placement of the pictures. You can put them anywhere and drag and drop them to where you want. Then, just print them on STICKER PRINTER PAPER!

What you will learn

- How to insert Online Pictures
- How to search for Online Pictures
- How to resize Online Pictures
- How to delete Online Pictures

Step-By-Step

Follow the instructions below to make stickers in Microsoft Publisher 2019

1) <u>Open Microsoft Publisher:</u>
   a) In Windows 10:
      i) Click the **Start** button OR in the Search box type **Publisher 2019**
      ii) Click on **Publisher 2019**
2) <u>Start a blank publication:</u>
   a) Click on **Blank 8.5 x 11"**

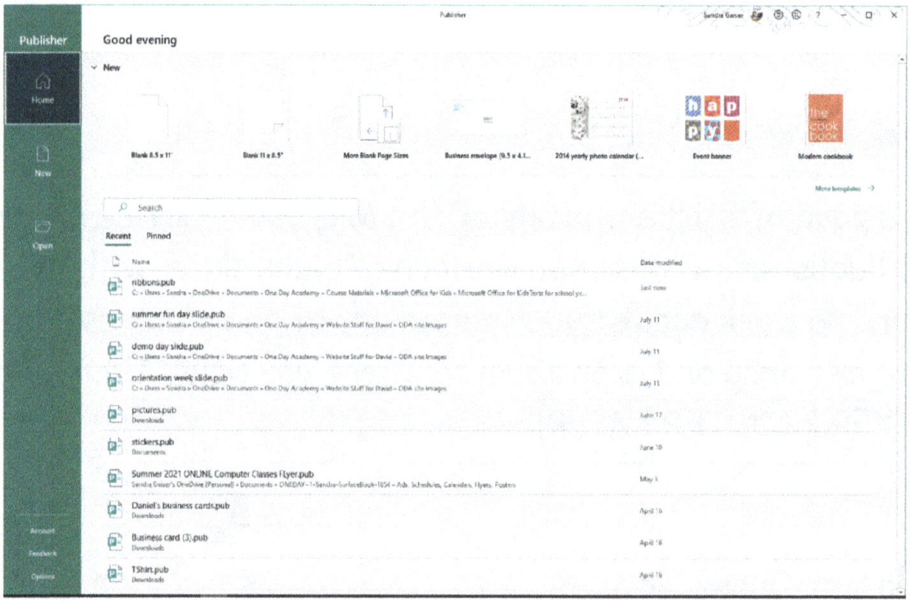

Microsoft Publisher 2019 opening screen

3) <u>Insert Online Pictures:</u>
   a) Click on **Insert** menu at the top
   b) Click on **Online Pictures** (to use Bing pictures)
   c) <u>Search for Online Pictures you want:</u>

i) In the **Search** box across the top of the window, type the name of the items you want picture of. The search works best with singular words (ex. *dog* instead of *dogs*). You must be CONNECTED TO THE INTERNET.

ii) Then press the **Enter** key.

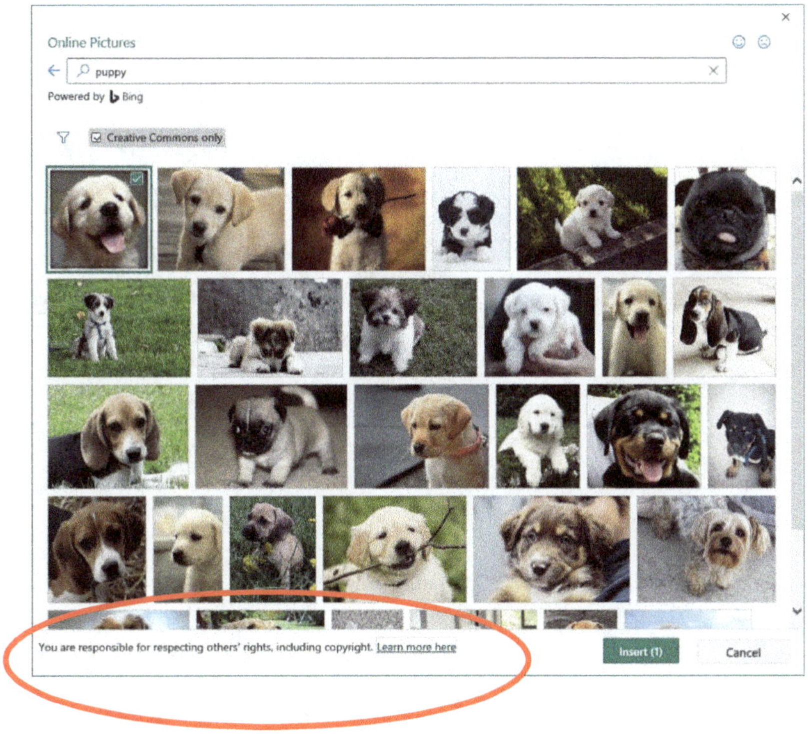

Creative Commons Only is checked by default. This means that the pictures shown have been uploaded to Creative Commons to be shared publicly under certain licenses.

NOTICE the note at the bottom-left of the search window that says: "You are responsible for respecting others' rights, including copyright. Learn more here." We will learn about Copyright in Lesson 21.

d) <u>Choose the pictures you want</u>
   i) Click once on EACH picture you want.
   ii) Then, click the INSERT button at the bottom of that window.
   iii) They will all insert on the right-side of your page.
   iv) Click the blank page to deselect the pictures.

4) <u>To delete a picture:</u>
   a) Just click on the picture and press the DELETE key on your keyboard.

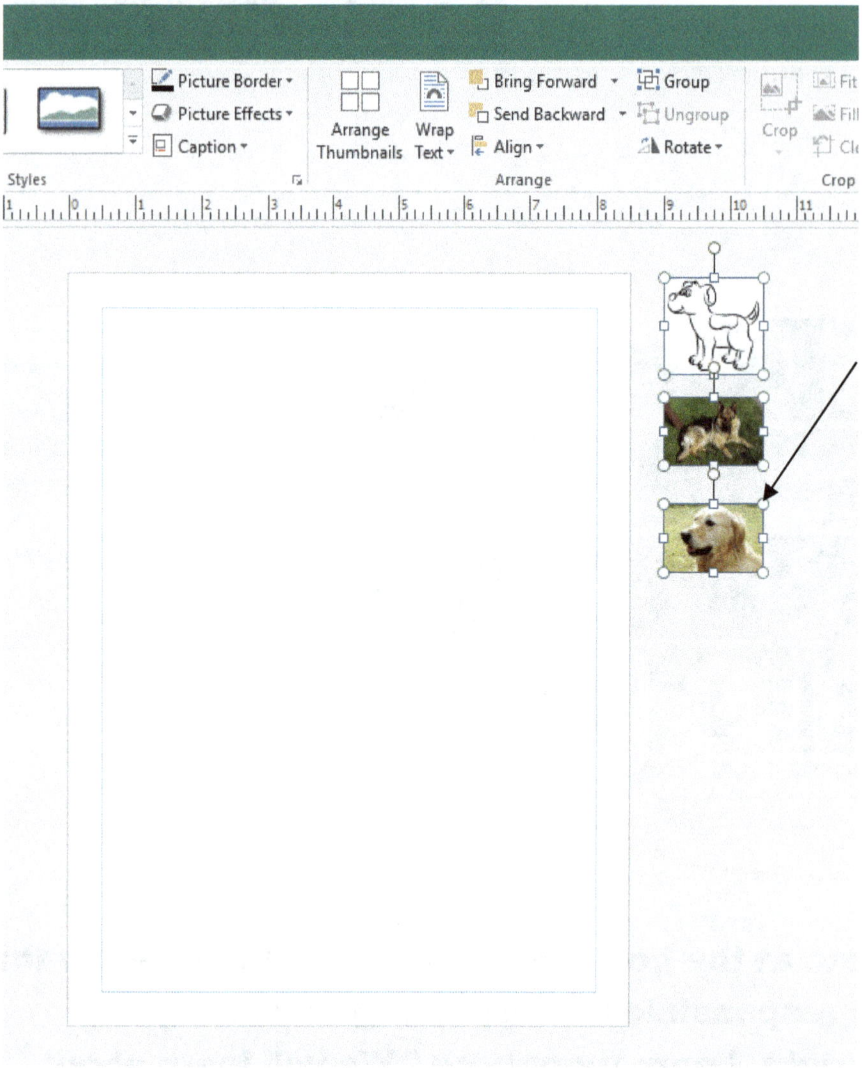

Notice that all the pictures are "selected" with little white circles around the sides of each picture:

5) <u>Arrange the pictures:</u>
   a) Put your cursor on a picture.
   b) When you see a 4-headed arrow, click and drag the picture around.
   c) Click off the picture when you are done moving it.

Move arrow

6) <u>To resize a picture:</u>
   a) Move your mouse to one of the 8 "handles" on the sides or corners.
   b) Hover your mouse over the circle handles on the corners.
   c) You will get a double-headed arrow, click and drag to resize.

Resize arrow

Rotate Handle: To rotate a picture, click and drag sideways.

Picture Handles

To resize a picture **PROPORTIONATELY** (Not squishing it!), pull **ONLY ON THE 4 CORNERS**. Not the square handles on the sides.

7) Insert WordArt (big, fancy words)
   a) Click on the **Insert** tab on the **Ribbon**.
   b) Click on the **WordArt** button: the blue "A" on the toolbar in the middle of the Ribbon.
   c) Choose a **WordArt** style (you can change the color later)
   d) Type in the word or words you want, like your name
   e) Click **OK**

Word Art button

8) When you have finished adding pictures & words, save the file:
   a) Click **File**
   b) Click **Save As**
   c) Type in Your name and project name (example: Nick's stickers)
   d) Click **Save**
9) Print your sticker sheet:
   a) Click **File**
   b) Click **Print** (make sure you have your special STICKER paper in the printer the right way!)
   c) Click **Print**

Lesson 2 Practice

Day 1

1. Follow the steps at home and make a set of stickers for someone in your family or a friend.

2. Print them out on sticker paper.

3. Give them to your family & friends!

Lesson Review:

1. What are Online Pictures?

   ____

2. What do you do to insert Online Pictures into your document?

   ____

3. Which resize handles do you pull on to NOT squish your pictures?

   ____

Planning for our next lesson:

Please read over this with your parent or guardian before our next class and sign it:

1. **We will take apart a computer in the next class. We will not put it back together.**
2. **The teacher will bring some computers and tools to class to take them apart.**
3. **You may bring an old computer to class if you want to take it apart. But remember, we will destroy it.**
4. **To be safe, we will wear gloves.**
5. **We will not break any pieces off. All parts will be removed properly.**
6. **You may bring home a piece of the computers.**
7. **I will follow the teacher's directions and be safe.**

____

Student signature

8. **My student has permission to take apart a computer in class.**

____

Parent / Guardian signature

Lesson

3

3-Take apart a computer & see what's inside

Let's look inside a computer!

About Our Project

We are going to take apart a computer to see what the parts look like and how they connect to each and how they work together. ONLY WORK WITH AN ADULT NEXT TO YOU ON THIS PROJECT!

What you will learn

- How to carefully take a part a computer
- What parts you can touch safely
- What parts you need to not take apart
- What to do the scrap parts when finished

Parts of the Computer System

Name: ____________________

Label the parts of the computer system with the letters given below:

Match the term on the left with the definition on the right:

a. Monitor	____a hand-operated electronic device that controls the coordinates of a cursor on your computer screen as you move it around
b. Keyboard	____ includes the chassis, microprocessor, main memory, bus, and ports
c. Mouse	____a smooth place for the mouse to move on
d. Mouse pad	____shows what is typed with the keyboard
e. System unit	____reads from and writes data to CDs & DVDs
f. CD/DVD drives	____places to connect USB devices: flash drives, printers
g. USB ports	____allows user to type input into the computer
h. SD card ports	____plays sounds from the computer
i. Printer	____connects the computer to the internet
j. Speaker	____places to insert a secure digital card from a camera or cell phone
k. Modem	____outputs files and screen content to paper

Step-By-Step

Follow the instructions below to take apart a computer safely. Never do this alone.

ONLY DO THIS WITH AN ADULT WORKING WITH YOU. NEVER TOUCH YOUR EYES WHILE WORKING.

1) Find a used computer that cannot be used again:
   a) Try asking local computer shops that fix computers for an old one they can't fix and will throw out.
2) Prepare yourself and your area:
   a) Put on thick rubber gloves - the insides of a computer can be very sharp
   b) Lay down a big plastic tarp or lawn bag to work on
   c) Gather screwdrivers of all sizes and kinds
   d) Get a large lawn and leaf trash bag to put all the parts when you are finished

You can find videos online on how to do take apart any model of computer - laptops can be challenging!

3) Take off the cover:
   a) Look for screws to unscrew to loosen the cover, levers to slide, or buttons to push

DO NOT UNSCREW THE SCREWS BY THE POWER CORD OUTLET. This is the Power supply and can house residual electricity. Never take this part apart, but you can safely remove it.

4) Carefully remove all parts inside the computer:

a) Unscrew all the screws to lift out the expansion cards and lift them out.
b) Remove the memory chips by pushing down on the levers next to the chips. The chips will simply pop up to lift out.

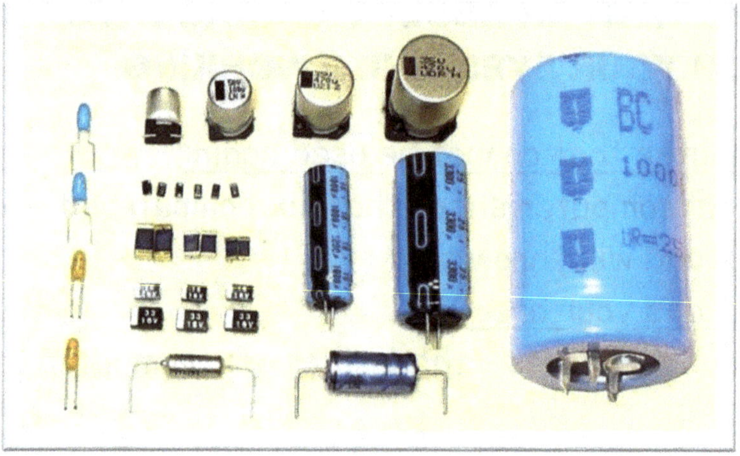

WATCH OUT FOR THE CAPACITORS ON THE MAIN & EXPANSION BOARDS. Do not snap them off, or a mild acid will make your skin itch if it touches you. If you do snap one off by accident, set it in your trash bag and wash your gloves with soap and water. Soap is a base that will neutralize the acid. Avoid touching that area again.

5) Examine all the parts:
   a) See if you can figure out how the part works and what it does. Use the pictures below to help you identify the parts:
      i) Did you find the memory?
      ii) Did you find the video card?
      iii) Did you find the hard drive?
      iv) Did you find the CD-ROM drive?

6) When you have finished, carefully clean-up:
   a) Put all the parts in the plastic bag.

b) Take the bag to a local donation store so that the parts can be properly recycled.

Lesson 3 Practice

Day 1

1. **ONLY WORK WITH AN ADULT NEXT TO YOU!**
2. **Find another computer to take apart, maybe an old laptop.**
3. **See if you can name all the parts.**

Lesson Review:

1. Where did you find the computer's monitor?

____

2. Did you find a USB port? If so, where was it?

____

3. Where did you find the computer memory?

____

Planning for our next lesson:

1. **To whom would you like to write a letter?**

   Their name: ____

2. **Write down YOUR mailing address here:**
   House or building number, street name & apartment number:

   ____ Apt. _________

   City: __________________ State: _______Zip code: __________

3. **What are some things you would like to ask them?** Some ideas are: How are you? How are you feeling? What are you doing for break this year? Is anything exciting happened to you since we last talked?

   ____

   ____

   ____

4. **What are some things you would like to tell them?** Some ideas are: "I am going on vacation to..." "I have accomplished this..." "I am taking a computer class this year, and I have learned to..."

   ____

   ____

   ____

Lesson
4

4-The Friendly Letter in Word

A friendly letter is a nice way to brighten someone's day!

About Our Project

We are going to write a letter to someone far away and mail it to them AFTER the next 3 lessons. Don't mail it until we're done with all 3 lessons!

What you will learn

- How write a friendly letter in Word
- How to show non-printing characters with Show/Hide
- How to line up text with tabs
- How to float pictures in a text document

What is Microsoft Word

Microsoft Word is **a word processor**, which means it **"processes" or handles words on paper** for us. It takes the keys you press on the keyboard and turns them into letters on the screen which can be printed on paper. Wouldn't it just be easier to write directly on a piece of paper? Well, not it you had to make changes or correct mistakes, then you would have to **rewrite on a new piece of paper**. Plus, it makes it very easy to make of copies of your work.

Five Parts of a Friendly Letter

There are 5 parts to a friendly letter:

1) **Heading**: This is where we type our address so the person can write back to us. This includes the sender's address (so the person can write you back!) and the date the letter is being written.

2) **Greeting**: This is where we greet the person. This includes a nice word like "Dear" or "Hi" and the name of the person to whom you are writing and then a comma.

3) **Body**: This is the middle part of the letter that tells all you want to say to that person and even pictures!

4) **Closing**: This is where we say "Goodbye" with words like: Your friend, Your granddaughter, Your nephew, Your niece, and then a comma.

5) **Signature**: This is where we actually sign our name on the letter with a pen once we have printed it out. It adds a nice personal touch. It's considered friendlier to sign it with a pen instead of typing your name.

The picture below shows where these parts are written in the letter.

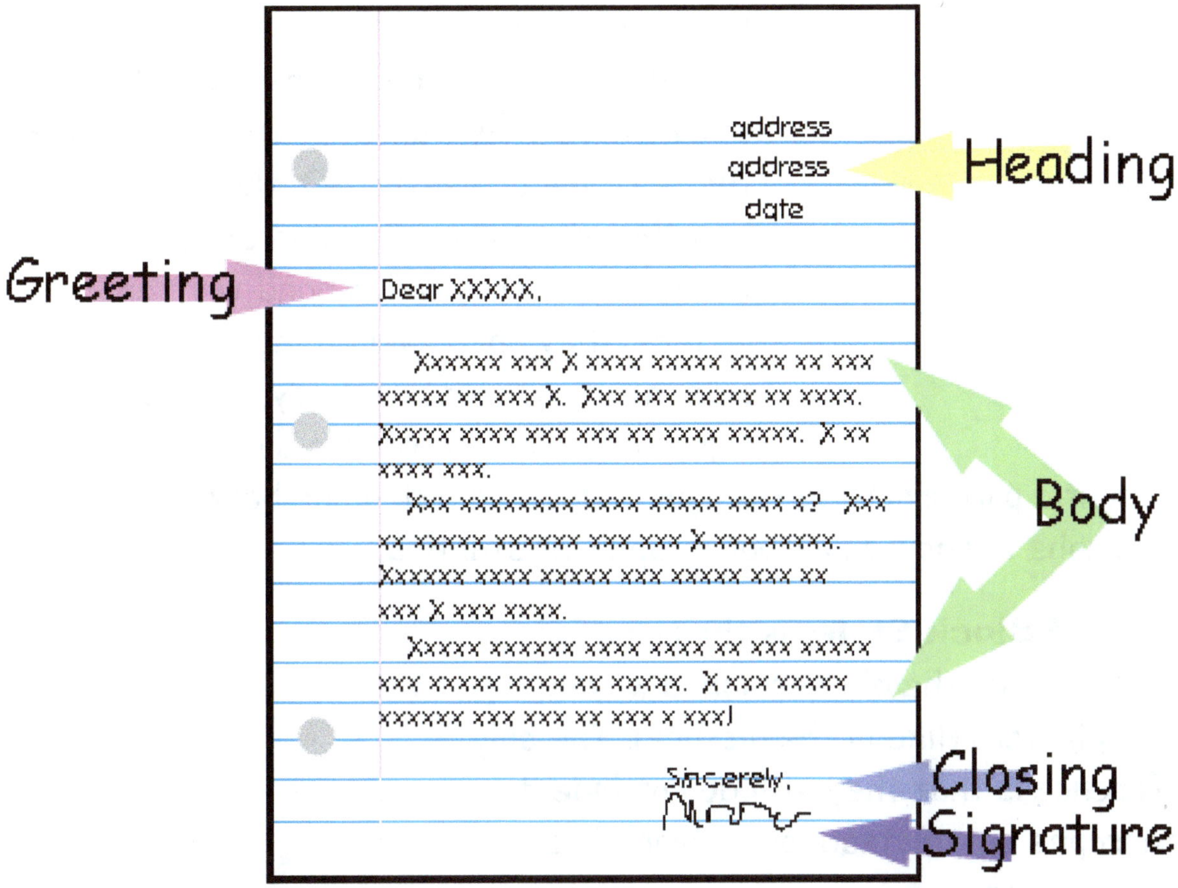

Image source: Mary Rizzo, Walter L. Parsley Elementary School, website: http://www.nhcs.k12.nc.us/parsley/curriculum/postal/envelope.html

Block Style vs. Modified Block Style vs. Traditional Style

Block Style

Block Style was developed after the invention of the computer. Many people had to write letters on the computer, but **few people knew how to move the text over** where they wanted it or how to make the text line up neatly. SO, they changed how they did things! Instead of indenting the text like they did in hand-written letters, they lined everything up on the left side: heading, greeting, body, closing and signature. BUT people also did not know how to indent a paragraph, so they just added an extra line between the paragraphs to show a new paragraph was starting.

Modified Block Style is the name for what looks like the old-fashioned way of writing letters (like in the picture). The only difference is that they still do not indent paragraphs but, instead, put a blank line between them.

Modified Block Style

Traditional Style is the name for what looks like the old-fashioned way of writing, like in the picture of our Friendly Letter.

Show/Hide button ¶

The **Show/Hide button** turns on and off the ability to see the non-printing characters in Microsoft Word. It's on the Home Tab in the Paragraph group. Since the computer can't understand "nothing", it uses a symbol to represent the different kinds of "blank" in a document: ➔ means a Tab, · means a space, and ¶ (called a **pilcrow**) means a new paragraph.

> ¶ **Paragraph sign** (from the Greek paragraphos, 'to write beside' or 'written beside') is a self-contained unit of a discourse in writing dealing with a particular point or idea.
>
> Paragraphs consist of one or more sentences. The start of a paragraph is indicated by beginning on a new line. Sometimes the first line is indented. At various times the beginning of a paragraph has been indicated by the pilcrow: ¶.
>
> The pilcrow symbol ¶, also called the paragraph mark, paragraph sign, paraph, or alinea (Latin: a linea, 'off the line'), is a typographical character commonly used to denote individual paragraphs.
>
> The pilcrow can be used as an indent for separate paragraphs or to designate a new paragraph in one long piece of copy, as Eric Gill did in his 1930s book, An Essay on Typography. The pilcrow was used in the Middle Ages to mark a new train of thought, before the convention of physically discrete paragraphs was a common practice.

Source: FSymbols-Computer Text Symbols http://fsymbols.com/computer/paragraph/

Lining up Text with Tabs

Sometimes you need words to line up in a document. But **you can't do it by simply adding more spaces**. You used to be able to do this on typewriters because all the letters were mono-spaced (that means all the letters were the same width). But now computers are smarter and can make skinny letters skinny and fat letters wider proportionally. See below:

Bill	`Bill`
(Proportional font)	(Mono-spaced font)

So, always use **Tabs** to line up your text, like we will today in our letter.

Let's get started!

Step-By-Step

Follow the steps below to create a friendly letter in Traditional Style to someone who lives far away, such as a grandparent, aunt or uncle or a friend in another city, state or country.

1) Open Microsoft Word:
   a) In Windows 10:
      i) Click the **Start** button OR in the Search box type **Word 2019**
      ii) Click on **Word 2019**
2) Start a blank document:
   a) Click on **Blank Document**

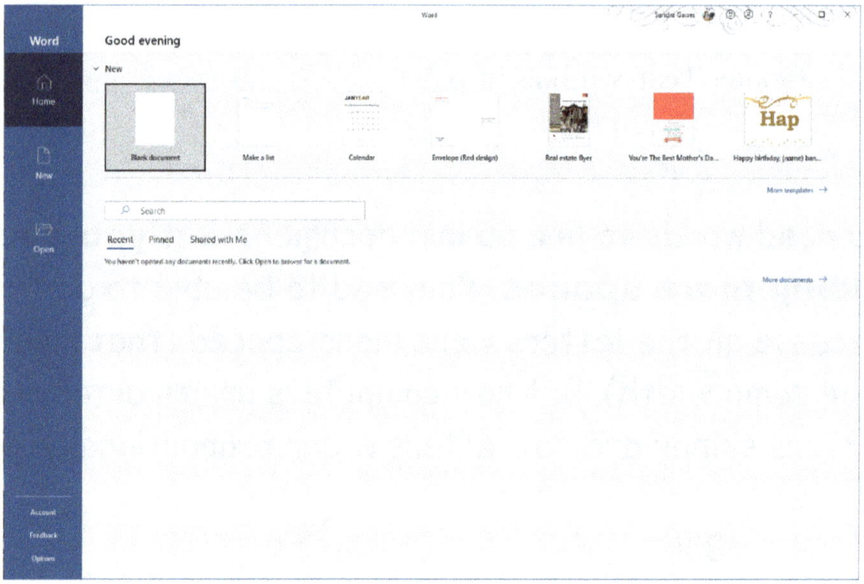

Microsoft Word 2019 opening screen

1) Type in the Heading:
   a) So we can see the **Tabs**, turn on your **Show/Hide** ¶ in the **Paragraph** group on the **Ribbon**:

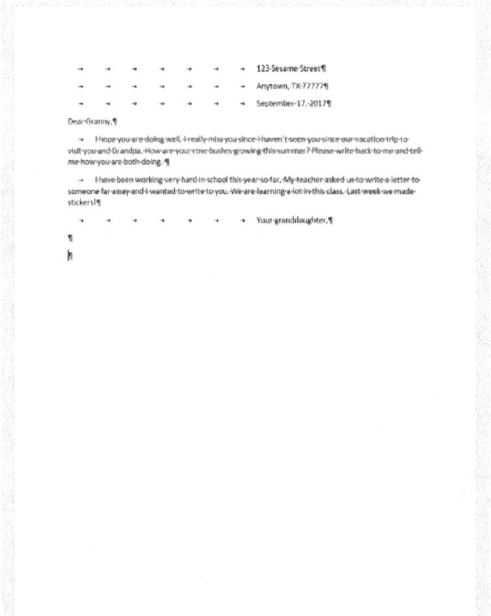

123 Sesame Street

Anytown, TX 77777

September 17, 2017

Dear Granny,

I hope you are doing well. I really miss you since I haven't seen you since our vacation trip to visit you and Grandpa. How are your rose bushes growing this summer? Please write back to me and tell me how you are both doing.

I have been working very hard in school this year so far. My teacher asked us to write a letter to someone far away and I wanted to write to you. We are learning a lot in this class. Last week we made stickers!

Your granddaughter,

b) Press **Tab** 7 times to indent the Heading.
c) Type in your street number and name.
d) Press **Enter**.
e) Press **Tab** 7 times to keep the Heading lined up.
f) Type in your city and then a comma and then your 2-letter state abbreviation.
g) Press **Enter**.
h) Press **Tab** 7 times.
i) Click the **Insert** tab on the **Ribbon**, then in the **Text** group, click **Date & Time** to insert today's date.
j) Press **Enter**.

2) <u>Type in the Greeting:</u>
   a) Type A kind greeting word like Dear, Howdy, or Hi
   b) Press the **Spacebar** and then type their name or names (For example: Grandma and Grandpa, Aunt Blanche & Uncle Bob, or Richard & Edna)
   c) Type a **comma.**
   d) Press **Enter**.
3) <u>Type in the Body:</u>
   a) Press **Tab** once to indent your first paragraph.
   b) Type your 1st paragraph. When you are done with a paragraph, press **Enter** to end it.
   c) Then press **Tab** to indent the next paragraph.
   d) Continue like that until you have finished the body of your letter.
4) <u>Type the Closing:</u>
   a) Press **Enter**.
   b) Press tab 7 times to line up the Closing with the Heading.

c) Type a nice closing word or phrase like Love, or Your grandson, or Your Nephew

d) Type a **comma**

5) <u>Leave room for the Signature:</u>

a) Press **Enter** 2 times to leave room for the signature you will sign with a pen after it's printed out. This gives it a personal touch.

6) <u>Add pictures!</u>

a) Click on **Insert** tab at the top

b) Click on **Online Pictures**

7) <u>Search for pictures you want:</u>

a) Click in the **Search** box and type in a single word like "dog" or "baseball". The search works best with singular words (*dog* instead of *dogs*).

b) Then press the **Enter** key

c) Click the image you want to select it

d) Click **Insert**

8) <u>Resize and arrange the pictures:</u>

a) Put your cursor on the picture in the middle.

b) When you see a 4-headed arrow, click and drag the picture around.

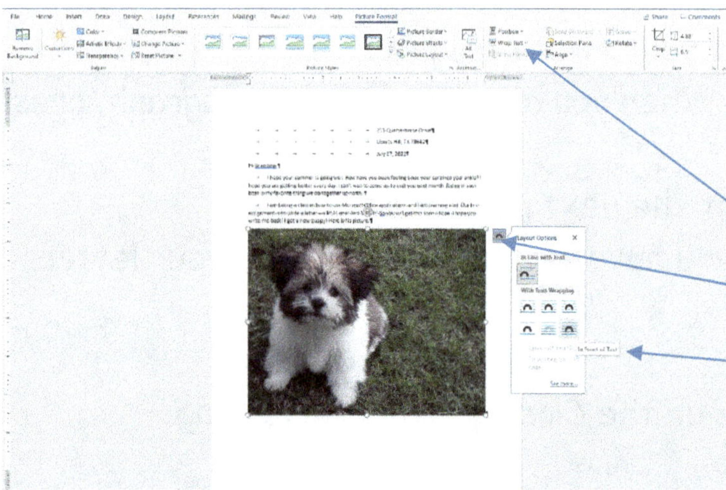

NOTE: To get the picture to float:

i) Click on the picture

ii) On the Ribbon, click the last new tab called Picture Tools Format.

iii) In the Arrange group, click on the **Wrap Text button**

iv) Choose **In Front of Text**

v) This will float your picture instead of trying to line it up with the words.

9) To resize a picture:
   a) Move your mouse to one of the 8 "handles" on the sides or corners.
   b) You will get a double-headed arrow, click and drag to resize.
   c) To resize a picture **PROPORTIONATELY** (not squishing it!), pull **ONLY ON THE FOUR CORNERS**.

10) When you have finished adding pictures, print it:
   a) Click **File**
   b) Click **Print**, click **Print**

11) To save the file:
   a) Click **File**
   b) Click **Save As**
   c) Choose the location where you want to save your file
   d) Type in Your name and project name (example: Nick's letter)
   e) Click **Save** button.

Lesson 4 Practice

Day 1

1. Follow the steps to make another friendly letter.

2. Print it out.

3. Wait until the next 2 lessons to mail it after we learn how to create envelopes and labels!

Lesson Review:

1. To whom could you write a friendly letter?

   ____

2. Name one style in which you can write a letter:

   ____

3. What are the 5 parts of a friendly letter?

   ____

   ____

   ____

Planning for our next lesson:

1. **Make sure you have the full name of the person you are writing your letter to (not Grandma, but Mrs. Smith):**

   Their name: ____________________________________

2. **Make sure you have their mailing address here:**

   Street number and name: __________________________

   City: ________________ State: _______ Zip code: _________

Lesson

5

5-Making Envelopes in Word & Publisher

Now an envelope for our friendly letter!

About Our Project

We are going to make the envelope for the letter we are writing to someone far away and mail it to them. **Don't mail it until we're done with all three lessons.**

You can make envelopes in BOTH Microsoft Word and Microsoft Publisher. Microsoft Word can do more than just put the letters you type onto a screen to print onto paper. It can also format and print envelopes. Microsoft Publisher makes envelopes with lots of design and style quickly and easily.

What you will learn

- How to use Word to make an envelope
- How to use Publisher to make an envelope

How to Address an Envelope

1) **Return Address**: Your address goes here just in case the letter cannot be delivered by the Post Office. They will mail it back to the Return address in case the person has moved, or the address is wrong or unreadable. *This is your address.* But DON'T TYPE ONE IN TODAY; we will be using our address labels for this in Lesson 6. This is placed in the upper left-hand corner of the envelope.

2) **Mailing Address**: This is *the address to which you are sending the letter*. It is placed in the center of the envelope in a nice, big, dark font. It is best to type the mailing address because letters are sorted by computers at the Post Office, and, if the address is unreadable, it must be set aside and sorted by hand. This slows down the delivery of the letter. You also must put all the parts of the address in the correct places, or the computer cannot read the address, and again, this delays delivery of the letter.

3) **Postage Stamp**: This is the sticker that you buy at the Post Office to pay for the delivery of the letter. Letters will not be delivered without the proper postage on them.

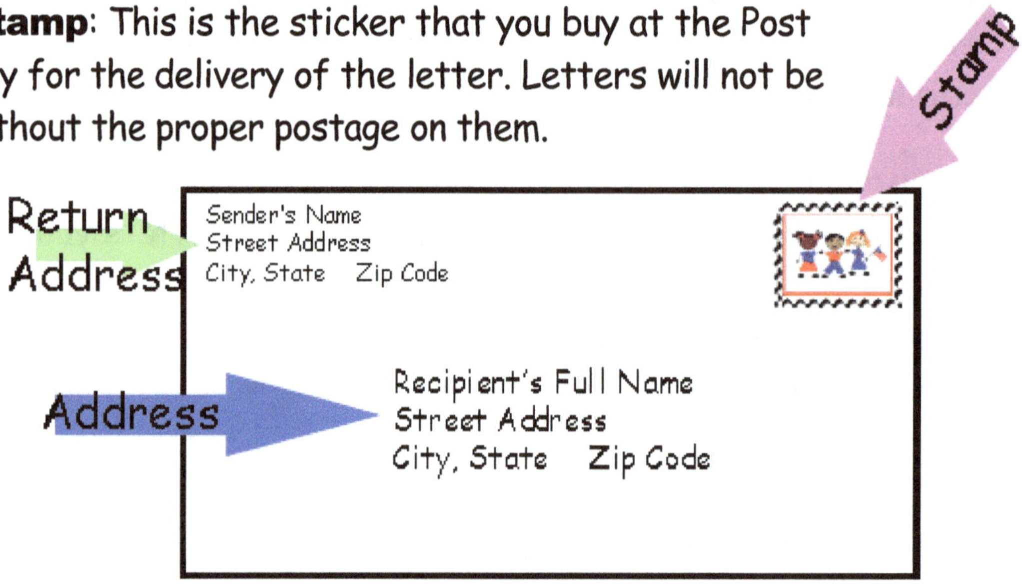

Image source: Mary Rizzo, Walter L. Parsley Elementary School, website: http://www.nhcs.k12.nc.us/parsley/curriculum/postal/envelope.html

Step-By-Step

Follow the steps below to create an envelope.

1) <u>To create an envelope in **Word 2019**:</u>
   a) <u>Open Microsoft Word:</u>
      i) In Windows 10, click the **Start** button OR in the Search box type **Word 2019**
      ii) Click on **Word 2019**
      iii) Click on **Blank Document**
2) <u>Start a blank #10 envelope (the size used most for letters):</u>
   a) Click **Mailings** tab
   b) Click **Envelopes** button
   c) Click the **Envelopes** tab
   d) Fill in the **Delivery Address:** box with the address of who you are sending the letter to
   e) Click **Add to Document**

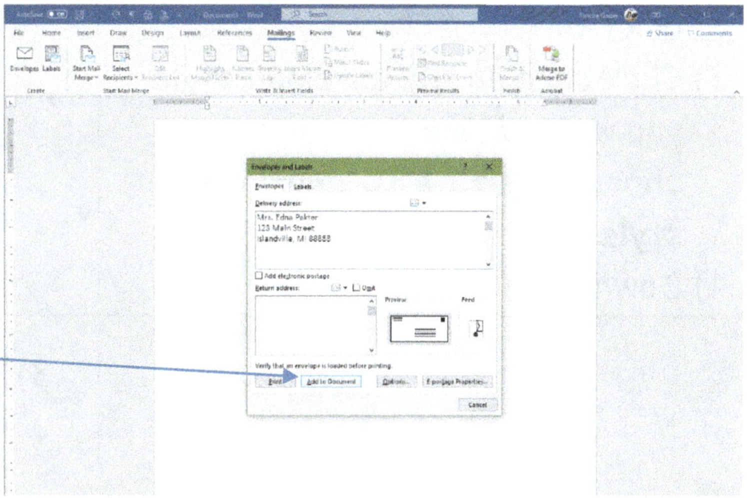

3) <u>Make it look nice:</u> You can insert clip art, change the font colors and font style and sizes!
4) When you have finished adding the envelope, print it:
   a) Make sure you load an envelope into your printer correctly (look on the printer for a picture)
   b) Click **File**
   c) Click **Print**, click **Print**

OR you can use Publisher for a fancier envelope:

1) <u>To create an envelope in **Publisher 2019**</u>:
   a) In Windows 10, click the **Start** button OR in the Search box type **Publisher 2019**
   b) Click on the **Publisher 2019** program

TO SEARCH FOR ONLINE TEMPLATES:

1) Click **New**
2) Search for **Envelope** in the **Search for Online Templates** box.
3) Click once on the envelope style you want. **Make sure you choose a size #10 envelope style.**
4) Download it.

TO USE A BUILT-IN ENVELOPE TEMPLATE – THERE ARE 53!

1) Click **New**
2) Click **Built-In** templates:

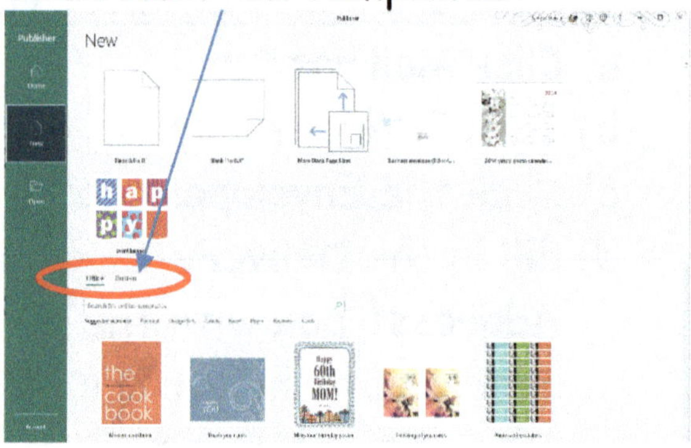

3) Click **Envelopes**

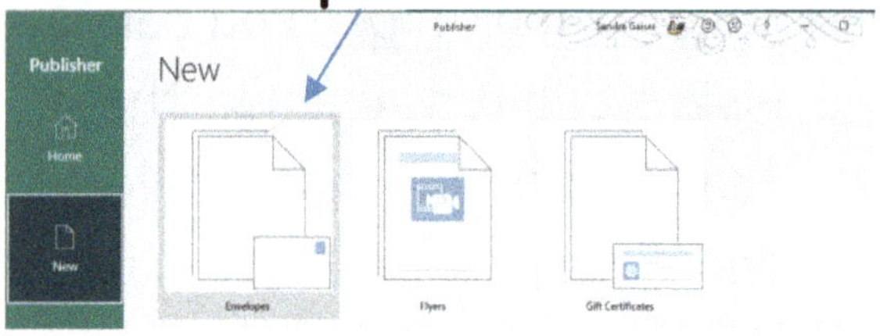

4) Click **once** on the envelope style you want (don't double-click or you will go right into the publication before you can choose your options)

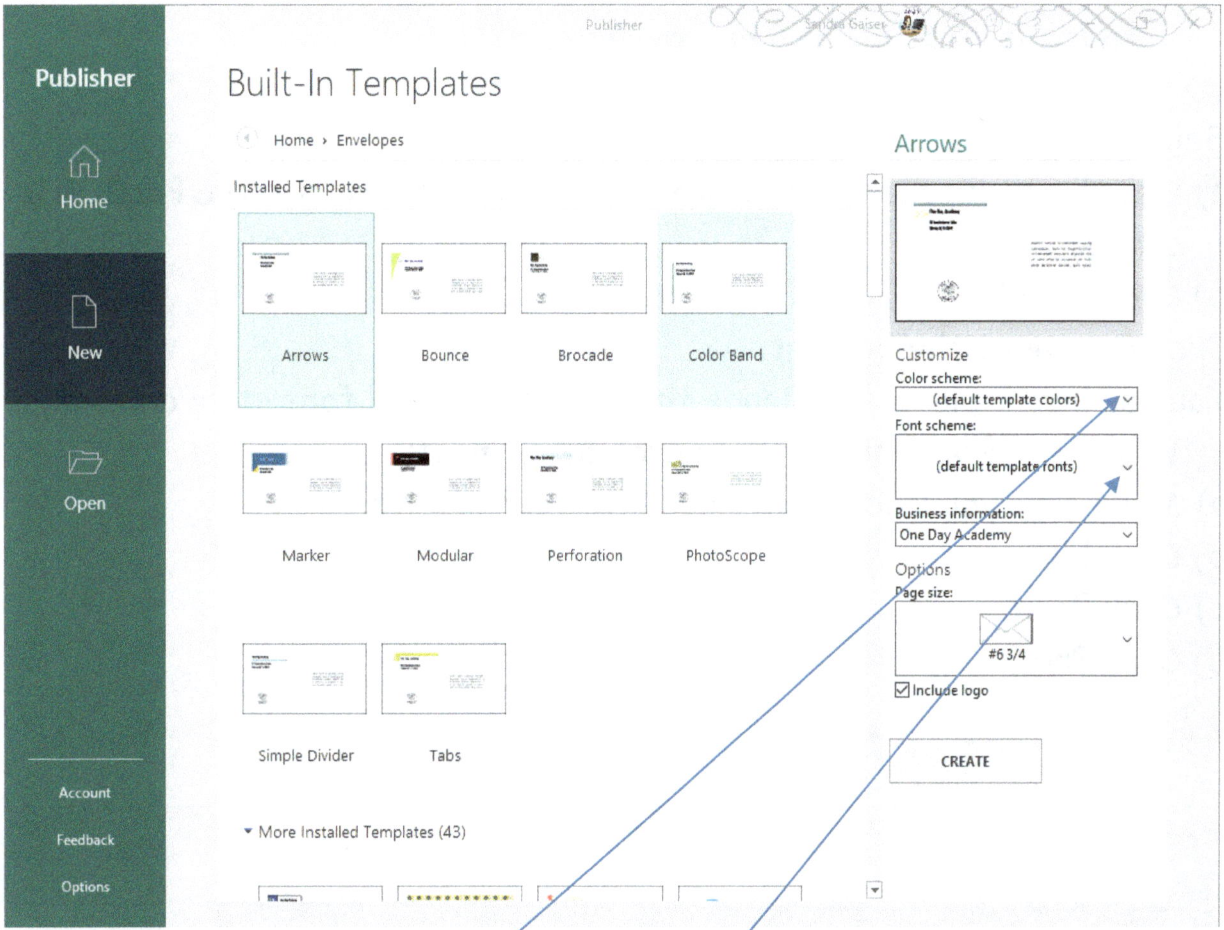

5) <u>Change the colors:</u>

a) Click **Color Scheme** and choose one of the colors schemes

To easily scroll thru the colors, click on 1 color. Then while it's highlighted use your ARROW KEYS to scroll UP and DOWN the colors!

6) <u>Change the fonts:</u>

a) Click **Font Scheme** and choose one of each or leave what they have

You can always change the fonts, too, later after you create it directly on the envelope.

7) Select the #10 envelope size:
   a) Use the task pane on the right, click under **OPTIONS**, the **Page Size** arrow
   b) Click on **#10**
8) Click **Create** at the bottom
9) You can insert pictures; change the font colors and font style and sizes!
10) When you have finished the envelope, print it:
   a) Make sure you load an envelope into your printer correctly
   b) Click **File**
   c) Click **Print**
   d) Click **Print**

Lesson 5 Practice

Day 1

1. Follow the steps to make an envelope for the person you wrote the letter for the last lesson at home.

2. Print it out.

3. Next week, place one of your address labels from class in the return address spot.

4. Put a postage stamp in the correct place.

5. Mail it and make that person very happy!

Lesson Review:

1. What is the Return Address used for?

   ____

2. What is the Mailing Address used for?

   ____

3. Where does the postage stamp go on the envelope?

   ____

Planning for our next lesson:

1. **Write down your full name and address for our return address labels next lesson:**

   Your full name: ______________________________

2. **Your mailing address here:**

   Street number and name: ________________________

   City: ______________ State: ________ Zip code: __________

3. What little picture would you like on your return address labels?

____

Lesson
6

6-Making Labels in Word & Publisher

Now some return address labels for our friendly letter!

About Our Project

We are going to make the small return address labels (size $\frac{1}{2}$ inch by 1 $\frac{3}{4}$ inch) for the letter we are writing to someone far away and mail it to them. **Don't mail it until we're done with all 3 lessons!**

You can make address labels in BOTH Microsoft Word and Microsoft Publisher.

What you will learn

- How to use Word to make return address labels
- How to use Publisher to make return address labels
- How to copy and paste

Review - How to Address an Envelope

Remember, there are 3 parts on an envelope that you need to know about:

1) **Return Address**: This is where your address goes just in case the letter cannot be delivered by the Post Office. They will mail it back to the Return address in case the person has moved, or the address is wrong or unreadable. DON'T TYPE ONE IN TODAY, we will be using our address labels for this later. This is placed in the upper left-hand corner of the envelope.

2) **Mailing Address**: This is the address to which you are sending the letter. It is placed in the center of the envelope in a nice, big font. It is best to type the mailing address because letters are sorted by computers at the Post Office and if the address is unreadable; it must be set aside and sorted by hand. This slows down the delivery of the letter. You also must put all the parts of the address in the correct places or again, the computer cannot read the address.

3) **Postage Stamp**: This is the sticker that you buy at the Post Office to pay for the delivery of the letter. Letters will not be delivered without the proper postage on them.

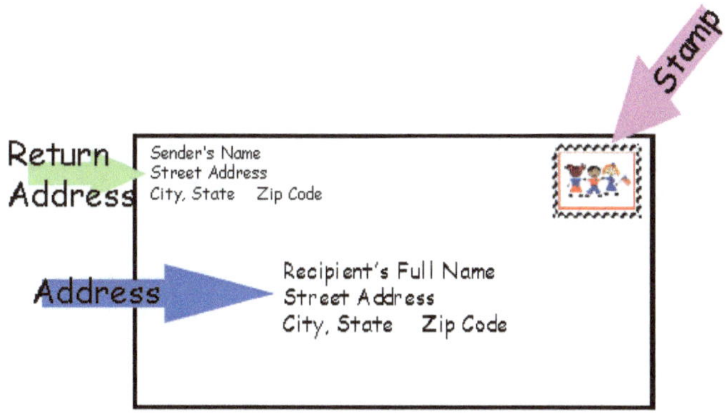

Image source: Mary Rizzo, Walter L. Parsley Elementary School, website: http://www.nhcs.k12.nc.us/parsley/curriculum/postal/envelope.html

How to Make Return Address Labels

There are 5 parts in your address that you need to know about so you can make your labels:

- **Your name**: Type out your full name. Make sure you capitalize your first name and your last name. This is the whole 1st line.
- **Street Address**: This starts with the number of you house or apartment building and is followed by your street name. Make sure to capitalize your street name. This makes the whole 2nd line.
- **City**: This is the name of the city you live in. Make sure you capitalize all words in it and place a comma after it. Don't press Enter yet.
- **State**: This goes right after the comma after the city. The Post Office prefers 2-letter state abbreviations, so make sure you know yours. Type it with 2 capital letters and NO PERIODS. The Post Office computers have trouble reading periods.
- **Zip Code**: This has 5 or 9 numbers and is specific to your city and state. If you don't know your Zip Code, look it up. It is very important to the delivery of your mail.

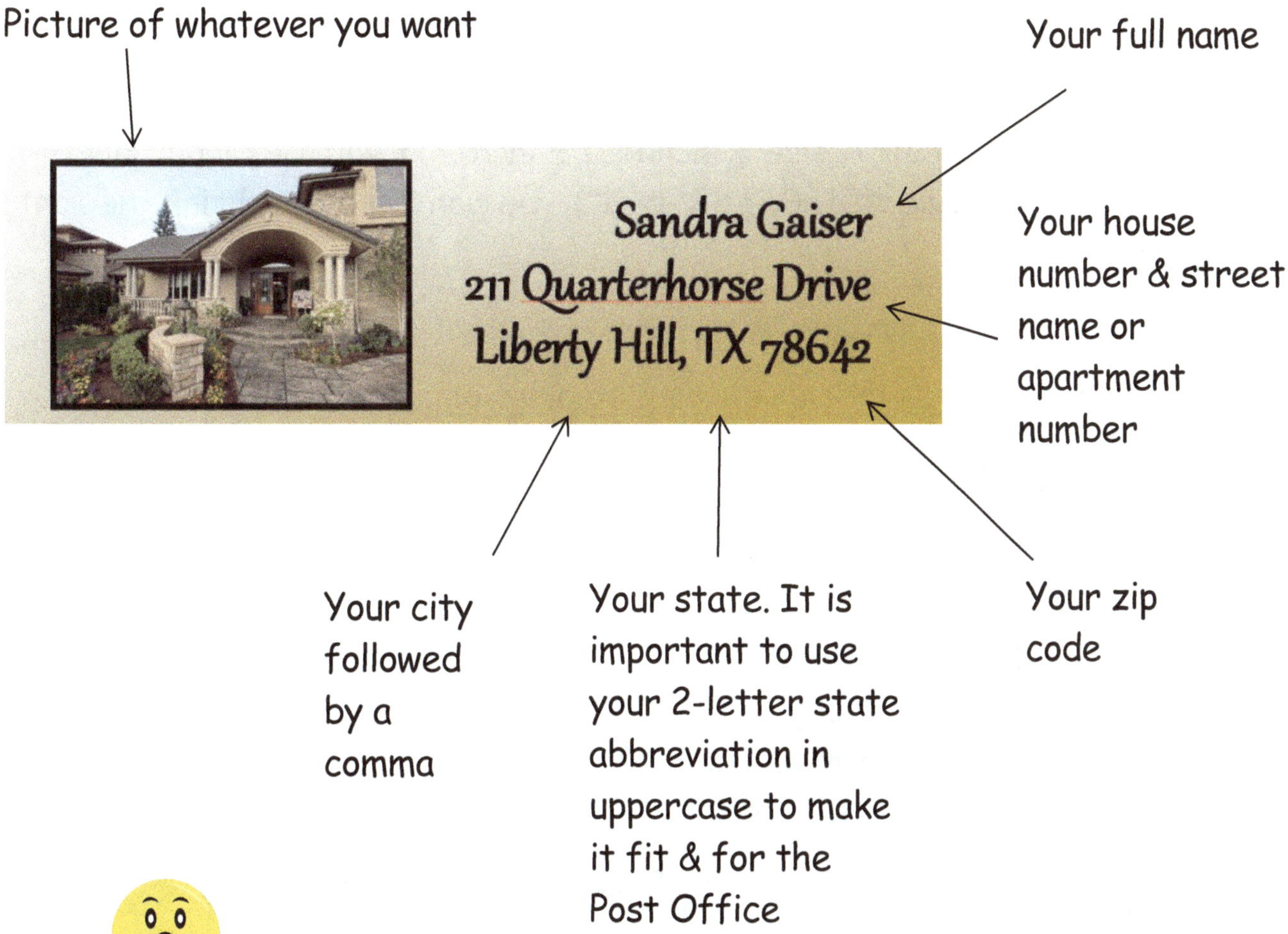

Don't forget to use proper capitalization!

Step-By-Step

Follow the steps below to create small return address labels (style #5167, size ½ inch by 1 ¾ inch). If you use bigger labels (like style #5160, 2.63" by 1"), you won't need to shrink the font as much.

To make address labels in Microsoft Word:

1) Go buy the address labels you want to print on
2) Open Microsoft Word 2019:
   a) In Windows 10, click the **Start** button OR in the Search box type **Word 2019**
   b) Click on **Word 2019**
   c) Click on **Blank Document**
3) Make a full sheet of labels:
   a) Click the **Mailings** tab on the **Ribbon**
   b) Click **Labels** on the **Ribbon**
   c) Type in your full name and address in the **Address** box
   d) Make sure **Full Page of the Same Label** is selected
4) Set the label paper size:
   a) Click **Options**

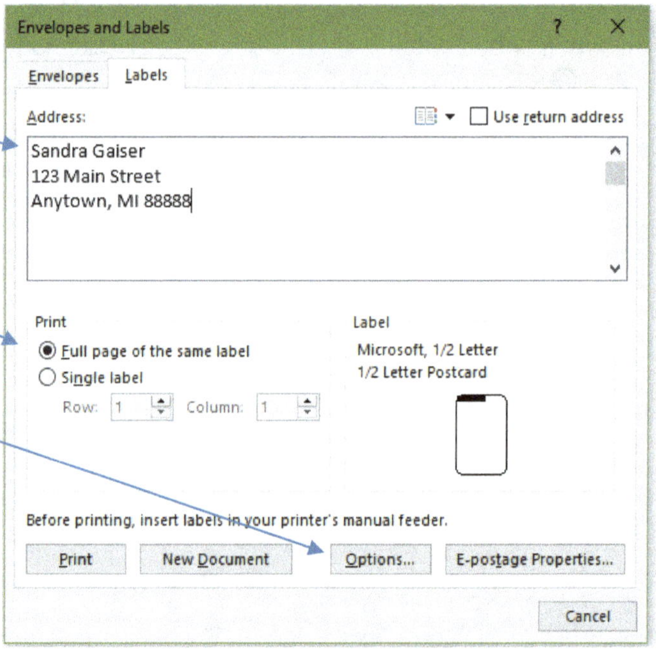

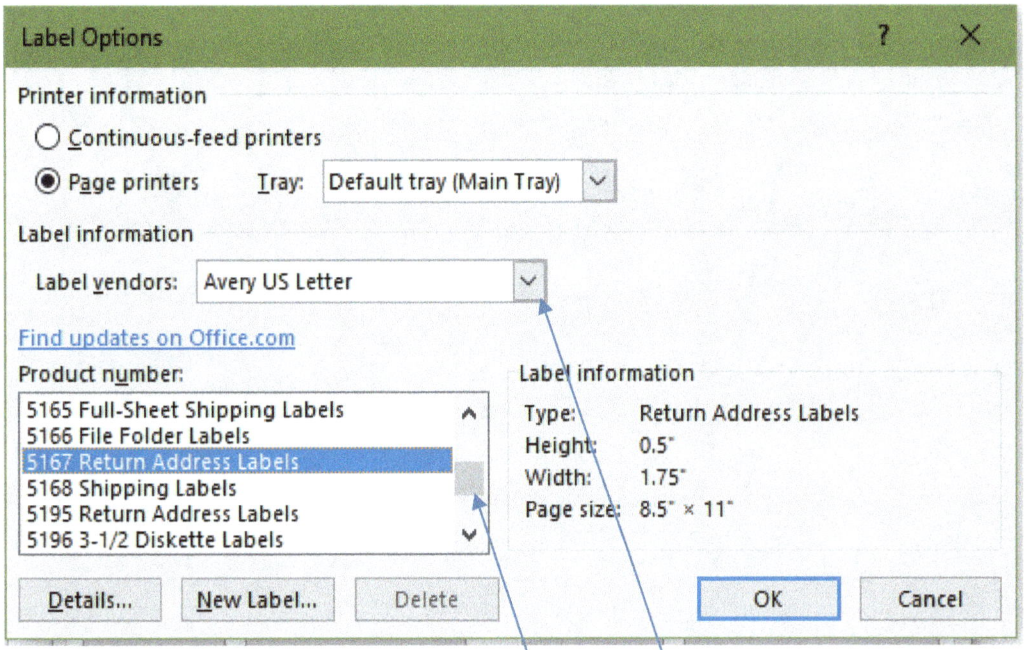

b) Under **Label Information**, click the little arrow and choose your **Label Vendor** name (I use Avery US Letter - be sure to use the label company on your package of labels)

c) Scroll down in the **Product Number** area until you see the label number on the package of labels that you bought (I use style #5167 - be sure to use the label number on your package of labels)

d) Click **OK**

e) Click **New Document** (Now you have a full page of the same label)

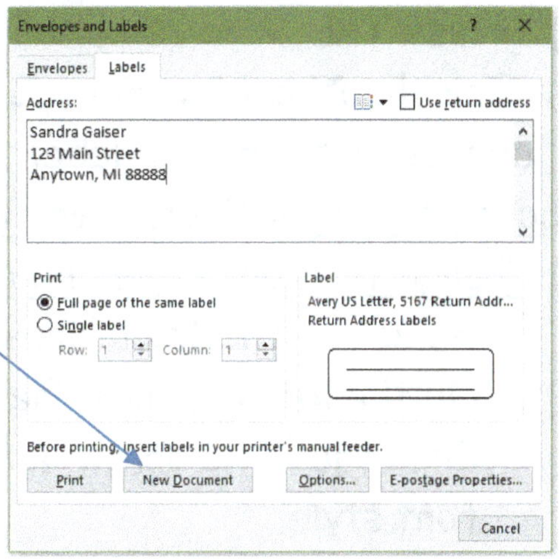

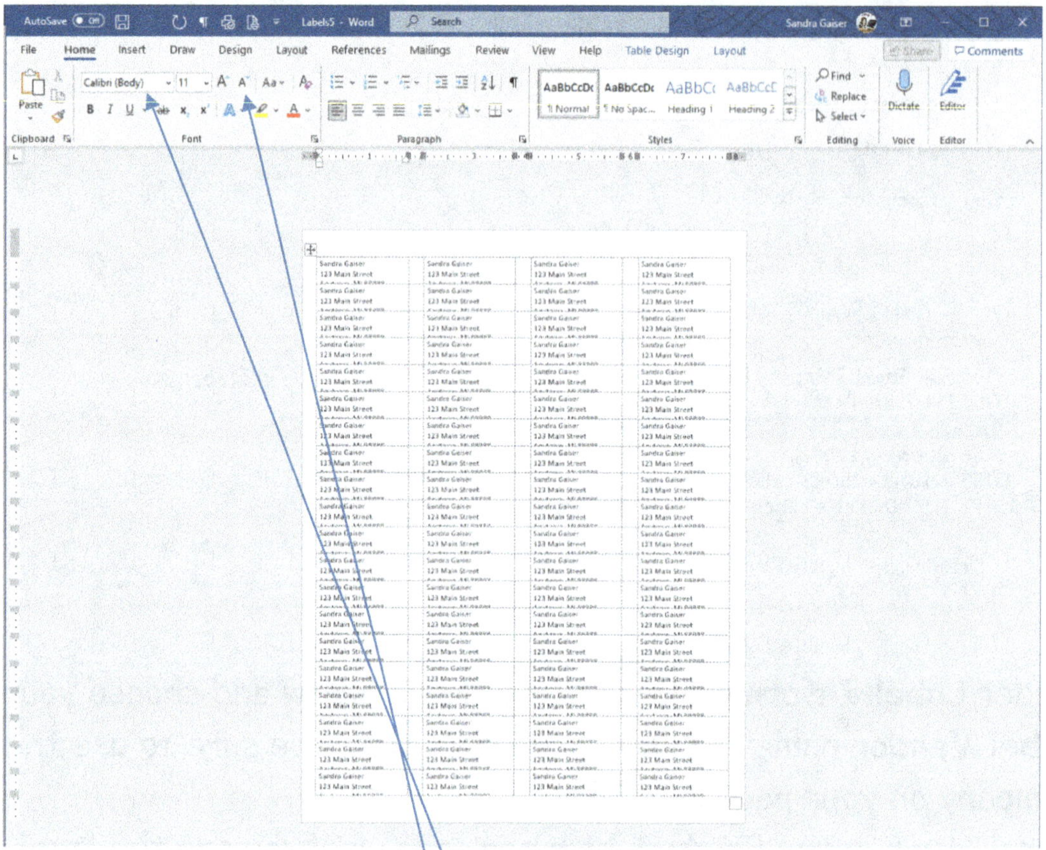

5) Shrink the font if all the text doesn't fit on each label:
   a) Press **CTRL-A** to select all the text
   b) Click the **Decrease Font Size** button in the **Font** group until all the address fits on each label.
6) Change the label the way you want it:
   a) Change the font style and color
      i) Select all the text (press **CTRL-A**)
      ii) On the **Ribbon**, click the **Home** tab
      iii) Click the little arrow next to the **Font** and scroll down to pick a font style
      iv) Hover over the fonts and watch them change on your label

    v) Try as many as you like, only the last choice stays. Click the one you like
    vi) Don't worry if your words don't fit on the label, just resize them like we learned in Step 5 above

b) <u>Now Try the Font Color:</u>
    i) Select all the text (press **CTRL-A**)
    ii) Click the little arrow in the **Font Color** button and pick a font color

c) <u>Insert an online picture on the left side of the label:</u>
    i) Click before the name on the first label
    ii) Click **Insert** tab
    iii) Click **Online Pictures** button
    iv) Search for the online picture you want, like we have learned, then click it, then **Insert** to insert it.
    v) Set the **Text Wrapping** to **Square**
    vi) Resize the clip art to fit on the right side of the label
    vii) Repeat for every label or copy and paste the clip art on each label

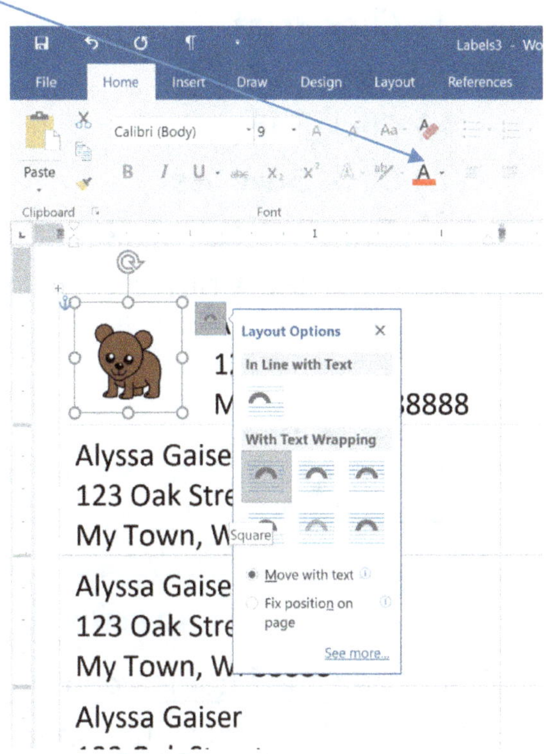

7) <u>When you have finished, print the labels:</u>

a) Print a **TEST PAGE on plain paper**:
    i) Make sure there is just plain paper in the printer
    ii) Click **File**
    iii) Click **Print**
    iv) Click **Print**

b) **CHECK THE LABELS:** Lay the printed paper over your labels and hold them up to the light to see if they match the size of your labels. If they do, continue. If not, make sure the number on the template you chose matches the number on the labels you bought.
c) Make sure you load labels into your printer correctly
d) Click **File**
e) Click **Print**
f) Click **Print**

8) To save the file:
a) Click **File**
b) Click **Save As**
c) Type in Your name and project name (example: Nick's labels).
d) Click **Save** button.

Microsoft Word can make labels, but if you want fancy labels, use Publisher!

To make address labels in Microsoft Publisher:

1) Go buy the Labels you want to print on (I use Avery #5167)
2) Open Microsoft Publisher 2019:
i) In Windows 10, click the **Start** button OR in the Search box type **Publisher 2019**
ii) Click on **Publisher 2019**
3) Open a featured label layout:
a) Click **New**
b) Click in the box to **Search for Online Templates**
c) Type in the label number on the package of labels that you bought (I use style #5167 - YOU use the number on YOUR label package)

d) Double-click on the labels that you want (if you want pictures on your labels, choose the **Pet Photo Return Address Labels**)

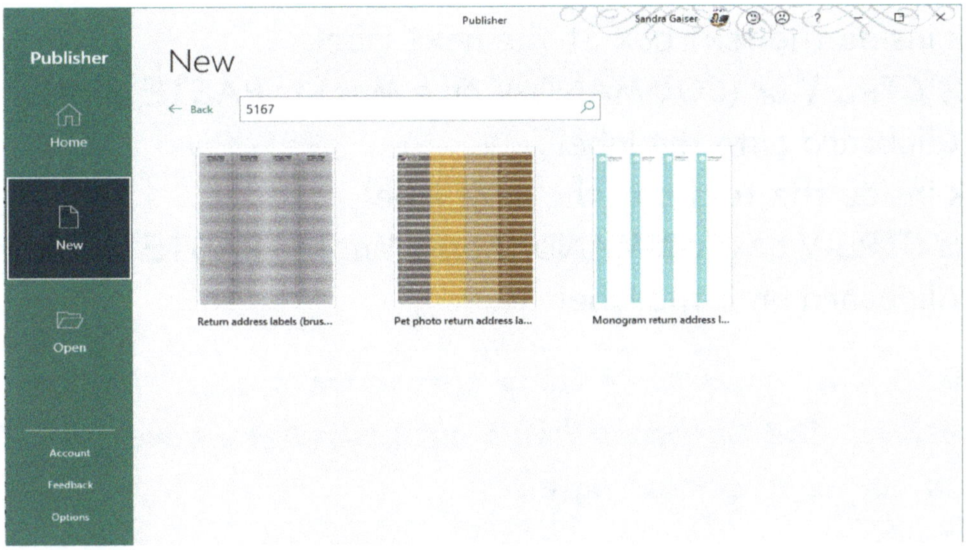

4) Replace the name and address with yours:
   a) Click in the first label on the words
   b) Zoom in using the Zoom slider in the lower-right corner
   c) Select & delete the name and address in there now
   d) Type in YOUR name, press **Enter**
   e) Type in YOUR house number & street name, press **Enter**
   f) Type in YOUR city name and a comma and space, your 2-letter state abbreviation in uppercase, a space, then your 5-digit Zip Code

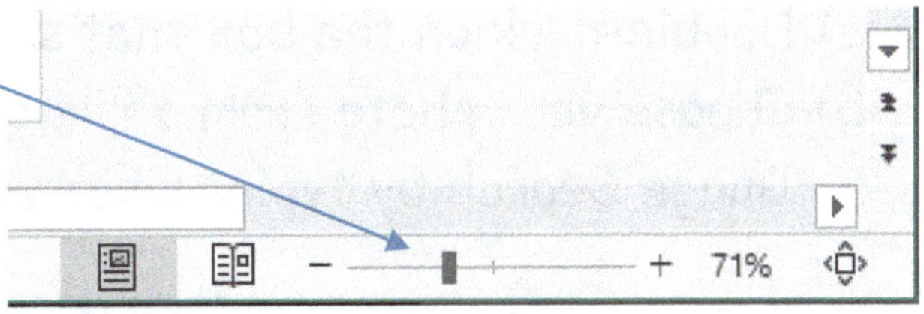

5) Copy and paste your name and address to each label:
   a) Select your entire name and address
   b) Press CTRL-C or (COMMAND-C on a Mac) to **COPY** all that text to the Clipboard

The Clipboard is an invisible place in the computer's memory that holds copied items to be pasted later.

c) Click inside the text box of the next label.
d) Press CTRL-V or (COMMAND-V on a Mac) to **PASTE** all that text in the Clipboard onto the label
e) Click inside the text box the next label.
f) Press CTRL-V or (COMMAND-V on a Mac) to **PASTE** all that text in the Clipboard onto the label

There is no need to re-copy the address each time to paste it. The Clipboard holds onto what you have copied until you copy something else!

g) Keep clicking on each label text box and pasting until all the labels have your address on them.

6) <u>Add a picture to each label:</u>
   a) Double-click on the box that says **Click to add photo**
   b) Choose your photo from a file on your computer or online from Bing Image Search by typing what you want in the Search Bing box.

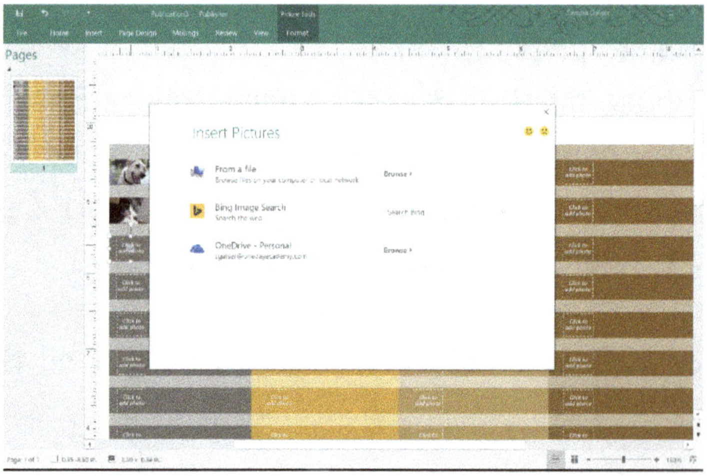

c) Double-click the photo & it will fit itself into the box automatically!
d) Add pictures to all the labels.

7) Change the label the way you want it:
   a) Change the color scheme (if you used a design template)
      i) On the **Ribbon**, click the **Page Design** tab
      ii) Click on the **Schemes** on the **Ribbon**.
      iii) Click a color scheme you like. Try as many as you like, only the last choice stays
   b) Change the font scheme
      i) On the Ribbon, click the **Page Design** tab
      ii) Click the **Fonts** button
      iii) Click on the fonts and watch them change on your label
      iv) Try as many as you like, only the last choice stays.
8) When you have finished, print the labels:
   a) Print a **TEST PAGE** on plain paper:
      i) Make sure there is just plain paper in the printer
      ii) Click **File**
      iii) Click **Print**
      iv) Click **Print**
   b) **CHECK THE LABELS:** Lay the printed paper over your labels and hold them up to the light to see if they match the size of your labels. If they do, continue. If not, make sure the number on the template you chose matches the number on the labels you bought.
   c) Make sure you load labels into your printer correctly
   d) Click **File**
   e) Click **Print**
   f) Click **Print**
9) To save the file:
   a) Click **File**
   b) Click **Save As**

c) Type in Your name and project name (example: Nick's labels).
d) Click **Save** button.

It's time to mail your letter!

1) Stick a return address label on your envelope
2) Fold your letter and insert into the envelope
3) Put a stamp on the envelope
4) MAIL IT!

Lesson 6 Practice

Day 1

1. **Follow the steps to make some address labels for your parents, siblings or someone close to you.**
2. **Print them out carefully.**
3. **Remember to print a test page first before you try to print on the labels.**
4. **Give them to them and make that person very happy!**

Lesson Review:

1. Which do you like better – making labels with Word or with Publisher?

____

2. What is a Return Address used for?

____

3. Why should you print your labels on plain paper first?

____

Planning for our next lesson:

1. **Write down your full name and address to make your letterhead in the next lesson:**

   Your name: ___________________________________

2. **Your mailing address here:**

   Street number and name:

   ____

   City: ______________ State: ________ Zip code: __________

3. **If you want to add your phone number and your email address, write them below. If you don't want to include these on your letterhead, leave this part blank.**

   Phone: ______________________________________

   Email address: _________________________________

Lesson 7

7-Making Letterhead in Publisher

Now let's make some personalized paper for handwriting letters!

About Our Project

We are going to use Microsoft Publisher make personalized letterhead or stationery for handwriting letters.

What you will learn

- What is letterhead
- What is included in letterhead?
- How to use Publisher to make your own personal letterhead

What is Letterhead?

Letterhead is another term for **stationary**. It's paper that is customized with your name and address for writing letters to people.

Mostly, it is used **for handwritten letters**, but it can also be fed into the printer and typed letters can be printed on it. You must adjust the page margins to do this properly.

It will have your name in large print across the top in a color and font that reflects you. Your return address will be printed near the bottom or side, so the person can write you back. It can have borders and pictures that reflect your style.

Review – How to Type in Your Return Address

- **Your name**: Type out your full name. Make sure you capitalize your first name and your last name. This is the whole 1st line.
- **Street Address**: This starts with the number of you house or apartment building and is followed by your street name. Make sure to capitalize your street name. This makes the whole 2nd line.
- **City**: This is the name of the city you live in. Make sure you capitalize all words in it and place a comma after it. Don't press Enter yet.
- **State**: This goes right after the comma after the city. The Post Office prefers 2-letter state abbreviations, so make sure you know yours. Type it with 2 capital letters and NO PERIODS. The Post Office computers have trouble reading periods.
- **Zip Code**: This has 5 or 9 numbers and is specific to your city and state. If you don't know your Zip Code, look it up. It is very important to the delivery of your mail.

Step-By-Step

Follow the steps below to create your own personal letterhead using Microsoft Publisher.

1) <u>Open Microsoft Publisher 2019:</u>
   a) In Windows 10, click the **Start** button OR in the Search box type **Publisher 2019**
   b) Click on **Publisher 2019**
2) Click **New**
3) <u>Check out the letterhead templates:</u>

TO USE A FEATURED LETTERHEAD TEMPLATE:

1) Search online templates for **Letterhead**
2) Click once on the letterhead style you want
3) Download it

TO USE A BUILT-IN LETTERHEAD TEMPLATE:

1) Click **BUILT-IN**:

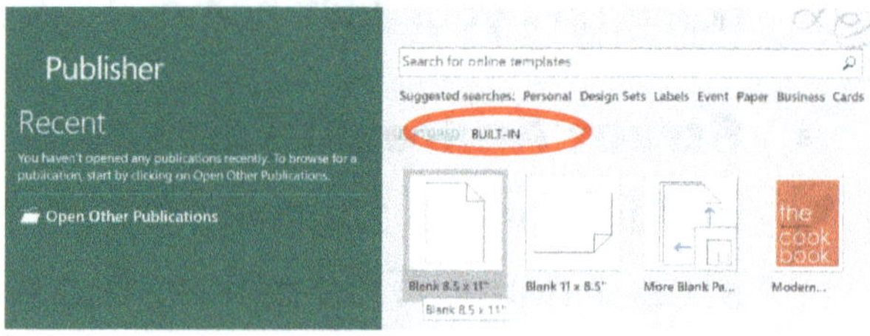

2) Click **Letterhead**
3) Click **once** on the letterhead style you want (if you double-click you won't get to choose your options)
4) <u>Change the colors & the fonts:</u>
   a) Click **Color Scheme** and **Font Scheme** and choose one of each or leave what they have
5) Click **Create** at the bottom
6) Uncheck **Include Logo**

6) Customize the letterhead the way you want it:
   a) Change the color scheme
      i) On the **Ribbon**, click the **Page Design** tab
      ii) Click on the different **Schemes** that you like. Try as many as you like, only the last choice stays.
   b) Change the font scheme
      i) On the **Ribbon**, click the **Page Design** tab
      ii) Click **Fonts**
      iii) Click on the font schemes you like. Try as many as you like, only the last choice stays.
7) Type your name in the main box that says BUSINESS or COMPANY NAME

Your name may already be on the page if your Microsoft Office products are registered in your name

8) Make your name big across the top:
   a) Select all the letters in your name and click the **Increase Font Size** button until it's as big as you like
9) Add your address, phone & email address, if you like:
   a) Replace the **[Street Address, City, ST ZIP Code]** line with your own information
   b) Replace or delete the **[Telephone] and [Email]** lines.
10) Insert a picture that says something about you:
   a) Click **Insert** tab, click **Online Pictures** button
   b) Search and insert the pictures that you want
   c) Make sure to keep the pictures small and off to the sides and top and bottom, so you leave plenty of room to write your letter
11) When you have finished, print the letterhead:
   a) Click **File**, click **Print**, click **Print**
12) To save the file:
   a) Click **File**, click **Save As**

b) Select the place where you want to save your file
c) Type in Your name and project name (example: Nick's letterhead).
d) Click **Save** button.

Lesson 7 Practice

Day 1

1. Follow the steps to make some letterhead for your parents, siblings or someone close to you.

2. Print out 2-3 copies of the letterhead.

3. Give them to them and make that person very happy!

Lesson Review:

1. What is letterhead used for?

____

2. Why is your address on the letterhead?

____

3. How many numbers does a zip code have?

____

Planning for our next lesson:

1. **Think of a story you would like to write:**

   Story Title: ______________________________

2. **Write down some of the characters in your story here.** What are their names? What do they do?

   ____________ ____________ ____________

   ____________ ____________ ____________

   ____________ ____________ ____________

3. **Where and when does your story happen?** Some ideas are: A forest, an airplane, a horse ranch, a spaceship, in America, in India, in Africa, in a hole underground, on a bus, inside a computer...

   ____

   ____

   ____

   ____

4. **What will happen in your story?** Most stories start with a character having a problem and then finding some way to solve it or something happens, and the problem is solved.

Problem: ____

____

Who solves the problem? _________________________________

How is the problem solved? _______________________________

____

____

Lesson 8

8-Make an Iconic Word Story in Word

About Our Project

We are going to use Microsoft Word to write a story using a combination of pictures and words.

What you will learn

- How to insert clip art in line with text
- How to use the Clipboard to hold copied items
- How to use the Clipboard to paste copied items
- How to delete clip art
- How to move clip art
- How to center a title

The Little Red Hen

Once upon a time there was a little red who lived in a little on the edge of a big . She could cook and she could sew, and she swept and dusted the little every day.

An Iconic Word Story

An Iconic Word Story is a story made with pictures. You have probably read books like these when you were very young. The main nouns are replaced with little pictures: instead of the word "house", you would see this . You can also replace some verbs like "run" with this picture: .

We will use online pictures to **provide the pictures for the major nouns** and some verbs in our story. Then we will use the Clipboard with copy and paste to insert the pictures where we need them.

Step-By-Step

Follow the steps below to create an Iconic Word Story of your own.

1) <u>Open Microsoft Word 2019:</u>
   a) In Windows 10, click the **Start** button OR in the Search box type **Word 2019**
   b) Click on **Word 2019**
2) <u>Click Blank document</u>
3) <u>Start by centering your title</u>:
   a) Click the **Center** alignment button on the **Ribbon** in the **Paragraph group**

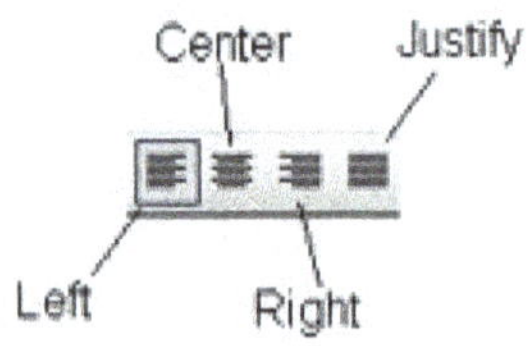

Text Alignment buttons

b) Type in the title of your story (or just the word "Title", if you are unsure what to call it right now – most stories are given their titles AFTER the story is finished)

c) Press **Enter**

d) Now return the alignment back to left by clicking the **Align Left** button

4) Begin typing your story

a) Press the **Tab** key on your keyboard to indent your 1st paragraph

b) Type a few words to start your story. You can start with ***Once Upon a time there was a…***

5) Choose the iconic pictures you will use:

a) Click the **Insert** tab on the **Ribbon**

b) Click **Pictures**

c) **Online Pictures**

d) Search for the pictures that you want to use to replace all the main nouns in your story (house, girl, boy, key, dog, cat, horse, skateboard, computer, etc.)

e) Click **Insert** to add the picture to your story

f) Click on each picture to add them to your document. Remember to click off the pictures before inserting another picture so you won't replace the picture you just added to your document.

Each picture should line up with the words – that is supposed to happen.

Don't worry how big the pictures are yet. Some might be very big.
And don't worry if you do not have all the pictures you need. You can add more pictures later as your story develops as you write it.

6) <u>Resize your pictures:</u>
   a) Click on each picture you have added to your document
   b) Using the **resize handles** (little squares around each picture), grab the **corners only** (or you will squish it)
   c) Drag until the picture is twice as tall as the words in your story.
   d) Make all the pictures about the same size.

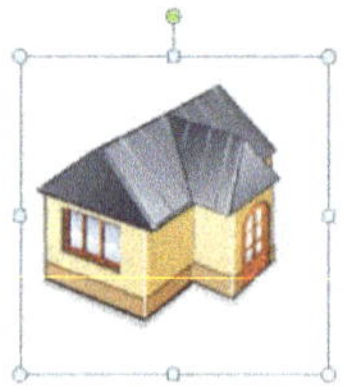

Resize Handles
(Use corners ONLY so you don't squish the picture)

7) <u>Making copies of the pictures:</u>
   a) Open your **Clipboard** by clicking on the **Ribbon**, in the **Clipboard** group, and then click the **Dialog Box Launcher button**. The Clipboard will open in a long window called a Task Pane on the left of the screen.
   b) Click on each picture one by one and press CTRL-C (or click **Copy** on the **Ribbon** in the **Clipboard** group) to make a copy of them in the **Clipboard** for use in your story.
   c) Delete the little pictures off the page in your story if you don't need them right now.

Dialog Box Launcher button

8) <u>Finish writing your story:</u>
   a) Type the rest of the story, pasting pictures where you need them by clicking on them in the **Clipboard**.
9) <u>When you have finished, print the story:</u>
   a) Click **File**

b) Click **Print**
c) Click **Print**

10) <u>To save the file:</u>

a) Click **File**
b) Click **Save As**
c) Select the place where you want to save your file
d) Type in Your name and project name (example: Nick's Iconic Word Story)
e) Click **Save**

Lesson 8 Practice

Day 1

1. Follow the steps to make another Iconic Word Story for a young child.

2. Print it out.

3. Give it to them and watch them smile!

Lesson Review:

1. What are the 4 text Alignment buttons called?

____

2. How do you open your Clipboard in Word?

____

3. What parts of speech did the pictures replace in our story?

nouns verbs adjectives adverbs articles

Planning for our next lesson:

1. **Can you guess what Microsoft Excel is used for?**

    ____

2. **Have you ever used Microsoft Excel before?** __________

    If yes, how? ______________________________

    ____

3. **Do you read a lot?** Yes No

4. **What is the name of the last book you read?**

    ____

Lesson 9

9-Make a Reading Log in Excel

A nice form to keep track of all the wonderful reading you will do this school year!

About Our Project

We are going to make a form in Excel to write down information about all the books we read this school year.

What you will learn

- What Excel is
- What a spreadsheet is and for what purposes it can be used
- How to add text in Excel
- How to widen columns and rows
- How to add borders to cells
- How to add clip art in Excel

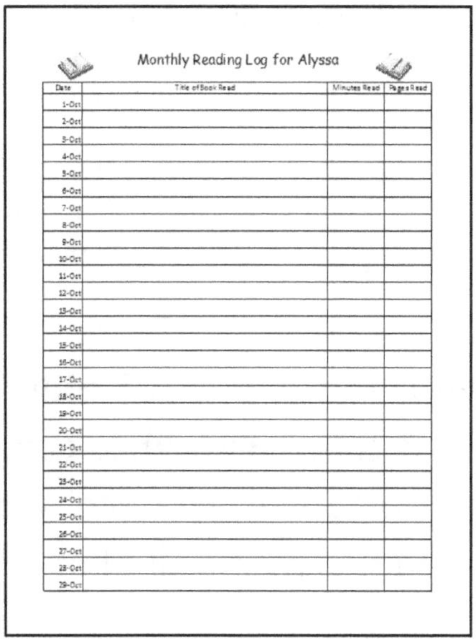

What is Microsoft Excel?

Excel is a spreadsheet program. A spreadsheet is a document with only rows and columns, like a big table in Microsoft Word, but much easier to work with and more powerful. **It is a good way to work with information that is best stored in rows and columns**, like:

- Names and addresses
- A budget that shows money coming in like paychecks and money going out as expenses
- Forms that you fill out
- Numbers that you need to add, subtract, multiply, divide or use with other math functions

Spreadsheets are **big**. In Microsoft Office 2019, one sheet can hold **16,384 columns** and **1,048,576 rows**. When you multiply those two, you can find how many cells (little boxes of information) are in one spreadsheet:

16,384 columns x 1,048,576 rows = 17,179,869,184 cells per worksheet

To see the last row, press CTRL-↓
To see the last column, press CTRL-→

Wow! That's over **17 billion cells**! And that's only **in 1 worksheet**. Each file is called a workbook and can hold more than one worksheet. How many worksheets in one Excel Workbook? Well, as many as your computer's memory can hold all at once. But, in the 2003 version, you could only have 255 sheets.

Imagine:

17,179,869,184 cells per worksheet x 255 = 4,380,866,641,920 cells in 1 workbook

OVER 4 TRILLION CELLS

OF INFORMATION CAN BE IN 1 EXCEL

WORKBOOK FILE!

That is a lot of information.

Getting around in Excel

- You can use the arrows keys to move safely any direction
- You can you the TAB key to left and Shift-TAB to go right
- You can use the Enter key to move down
- You can type the name of the cell that you want to go to in the **Name Box**
    - Just like in the game Battleship®, you name the column letter first and then the number of the row: A1 or Z800.

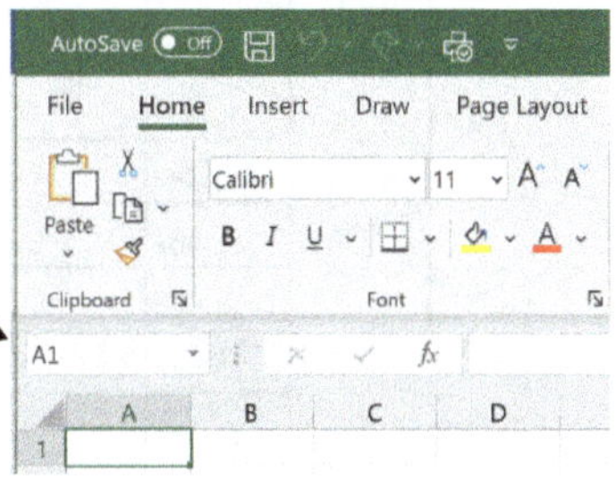

A Reading Log

We are going to make a Reading Log like the picture. We are going to track our reading by minutes, as well as by chapters or pages.

Monthly Reading Log for Alyssa

Date	Title of Book Read	Minutes Read	Chapters Read
1-Nov			
2-Nov			
3-Nov			
4-Nov			
5-Nov			
6-Nov			
7-Nov			
8-Nov			
9-Nov			
10-Nov			
11-Nov			
12-Nov			
13-Nov			
14-Nov			
15-Nov			
16-Nov			
17-Nov			
18-Nov			
19-Nov			
20-Nov			
21-Nov			
22-Nov			
23-Nov			
24-Nov			
25-Nov			
26-Nov			
27-Nov			
28-Nov			

Step-By-Step

Follow the steps below to create a Monthly Reading Log in Excel.

1) Open Microsoft Excel 2019:
   a) In Windows 10, click the **Start** button OR in the Search box type **Excel 2019**
   b) Click on **Excel 2019**
   c) Click **Blank workbook**

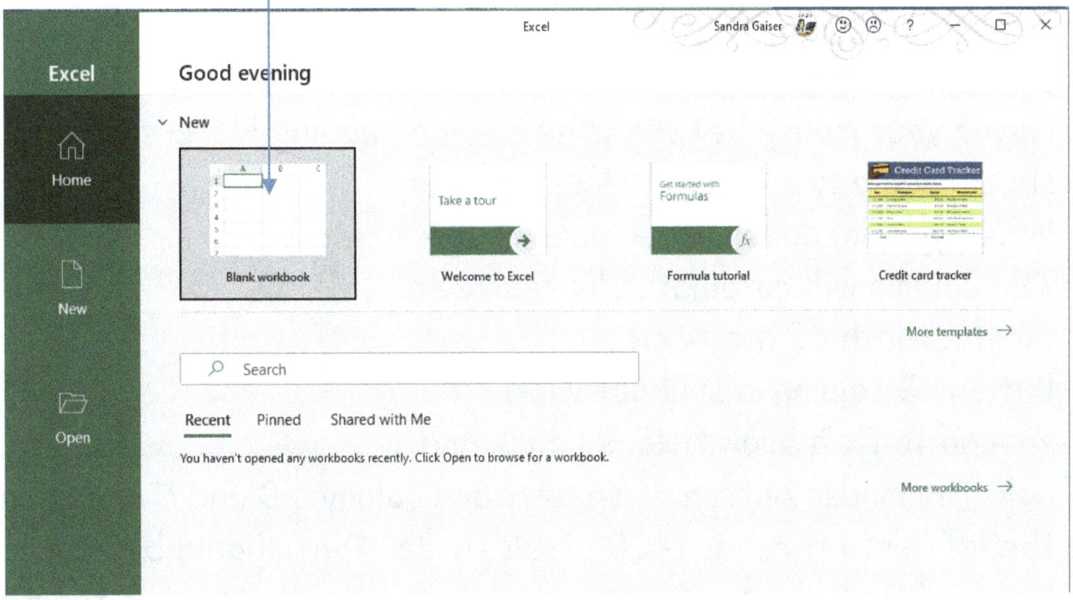

2) Title the reading log:
   a) Click on the very first cell A1
   b) Type **Monthly Reading Log for (type your name)**
   c) Press **Enter**
3) Now let's enter the column headings:
   a) Click on cell A3 and type **Date**.
   b) Press **TAB** on your keyboard to move sideways to cell B3.
   c) Type **Title of Book Read**.

d) Press **TAB** to move to cell C3.

Now we will type right on top of the words in this cell. Don't worry how thin the columns are right now. We'll fix that next.

e) Type **Minutes Read** or **Hours Read**, depending on how you want to track your reading.
f) Press **TAB** to move to cell D3.
g) Type **Pages Read** or **Chapters Read**, depending on how you want to track your reading.
h) Press **Enter** or **TAB**

4) <u>Now, to widen the columns:</u>
   a) Hover your mouse between the column heading letters B and C. You should see a two-headed black arrow.

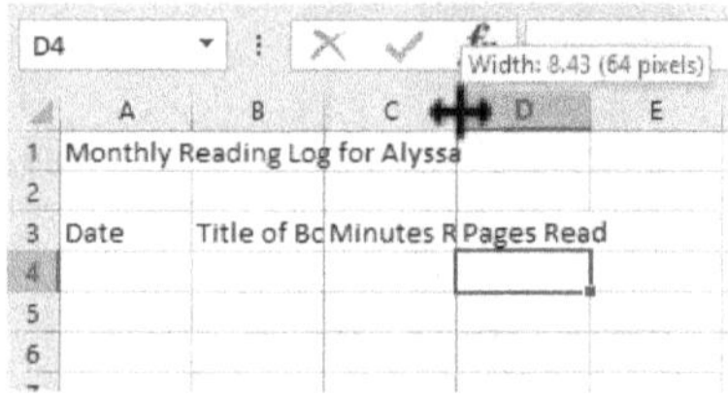

   b) When you do, double-click your mouse. The column will automatically resize to fit the width of the text.
   c) But the B column is still not wide enough to fit a book title, so click and hold the mouse button down between columns B and C and drag it to the left until it reads (400 pixels) wide. That should be perfect.
   d) **Don't widen columns C and D.** We will wrap the text in them next.
5) <u>Let's wrap the text in the column headings:</u>
   a) Click directly on the row number **3** to select the whole row. It will become shaded.
   b) Click the **Wrap Text** button on **Home** tab the **Ribbon** in the **Alignment Group**.
6) <u>Let's bold and center the column headings:</u>
   a) Keep row 3 selected. It should still be shaded. Click the **B** in the **Font** group on the **Home** tab.

b) Click the **Center** button on the **Ribbon** in the **Alignment Group** to center the text horizontally.

c) Click the **Middle Align** button on the **Ribbon** in the **Alignment Group** to center the text vertically.

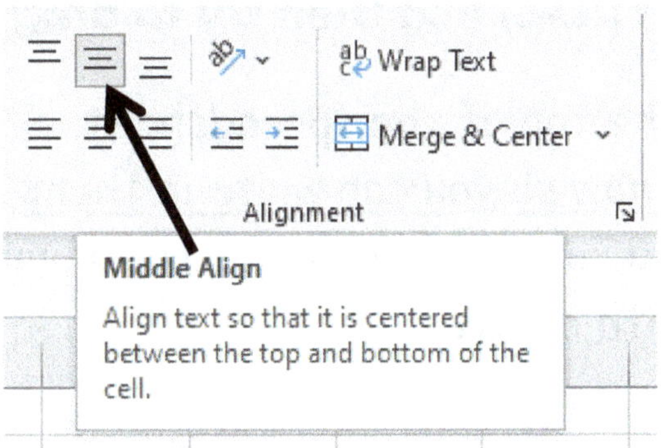

7) <u>If the text in row 3 is cut off on the bottom</u>, let's resize the row: put your mouse between rows 3 and 4 and double-click your mouse.

8) <u>Now, to enter the dates:</u>

   a) Click on cell A4 and type **Oct 1** (or the first day of any month) and press **Enter**. The date will change format to look like this: 1-Oct. That's because this date format is the default format.

   b) Now click on cell A4 again, and then put your mouse in the lower right corner. The mouse pointer should change to a little black plus sign (+).

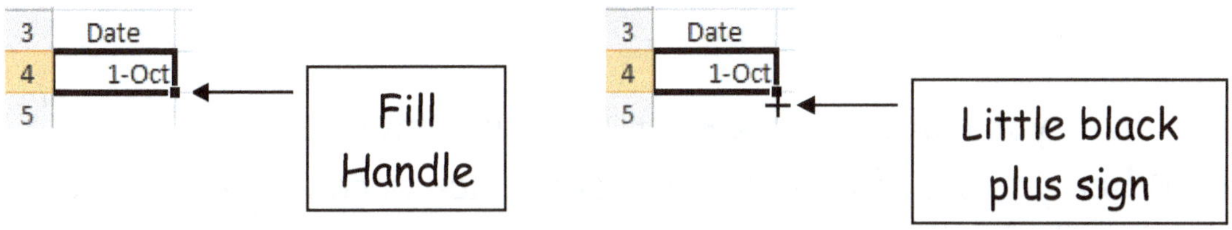

c) When you see that, click and hold your mouse button down and drag down about 30-31 rows until the date box says 31-Oct (or the last day of the month you are using). Then let go of the mouse.

If you scroll down TOO far, like to 3-Nov or so, simply KEEP HOLDING THE MOUSE BUTTON DOWN and move up until you get to 31-Oct (or the date you want). When you get there, THEN let go of the mouse. If you let go too early, simple click "Undo" (or press CTRL-Z) and then try to drag down again.

d) Scroll back up to the top of the spreadsheet.

9) Let's widen the rows now so you can write in them:

a) Select all the dated rows by clicking on row number **3** and dragging down to last row with a date.

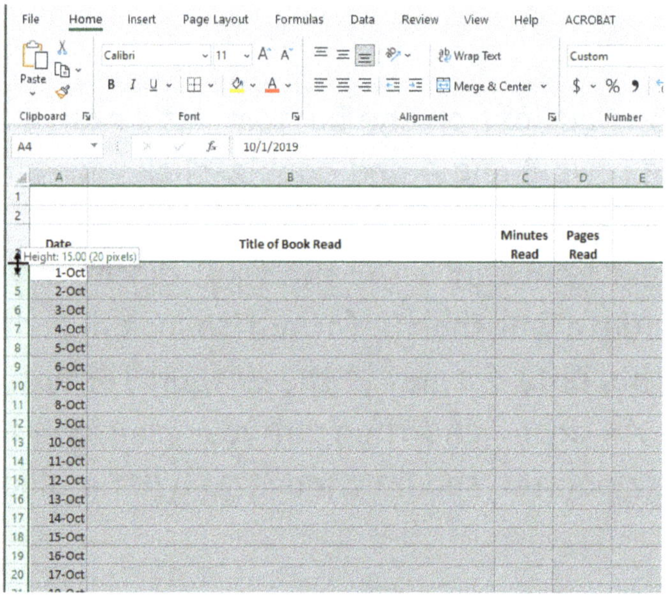

b) Hover you mouse between any 2 row numbers

c) When you see the double-headed black arrow, click and drag down *slightly* so all the rows will be 30 pixels wide.

   d) Scroll up and click anywhere to deselect everything.

10) Now take a look in Print Preview (Click the **File**, then **Print**).

11) What's missing? Lines! They are called **Borders** in Excel. Let's add them:

   a) Click on **File** again to get back to editing the document.

   b) Select all your dated rows and columns of your reading log:

      i) When your mouse is a white plus sign, click on cell A3, holding down your mouse button, drag over to cell D3 and continue downward till you reach the last row starting with 31-Oct. Let go of the mouse button.

   c) On the Ribbon, in the Font group, look for the **Bottom Border button** (□). Click the tiny, black arrow next to the box for more choices.

   d) Click on **All Borders**.

   e) Now click on **File, Print** again to see what it looks like.

12) Now to make the title nicer:

   a) Click on A1 and drag over to D1 to select the top row of the first page.

   b) On the Ribbon, in the **Alignment Group**, click **Merge and Center**.

   c) With it still selected, change the font style to something you like: (**Home** tab, **Font** group)

   d) With it still selected, increase the size (**Home** tab, **Font** group) (22 is a good title size font).

   e) Let's add some color to the top of the log: Click on A3 and drag over to D3 to select the top row of the reading log.

   f) On the **Home** tab, in the **Font** group, click the **Fill Color** button. Click the little arrow for more colors.

13) Insert a tiny picture of a book in the upper left and right corner:

   a) Click the **Insert** tab on the **Ribbon**.

   b) Click the **Online Pictures** button in the **Illustrations** group. Search for "book" & click on the image you want.

c) Shrink the image to fit at the top of your reading log. Copy and paste a 2nd picture across from it.

14) <u>Since you have 2 pages, you will want the title rows to repeat at the top of the second page. Here's how:</u>

a) On the **Ribbon**, click the **Page Layout** tab.
b) In the **Page Setup** group, click the **Print Titles** button.
c) Click the red arrow next to **Rows to Repeat at Top**.
d) Click on the row number 1, drag down to select rows 1, 2, and 3.
e) Press **Enter**.
f) Click **OK**.

15) <u>When you have finished, print the form:</u>

a) Click **File**
b) Click **Print**, Click **Print**

16) <u>To save the file:</u>

a) Click **File, click Save As**
b) Select the place where you want to save your file
c) Type in Your name and project name (example: Nick's Reading form).
d) Click **Save** button

Lesson 9 Practice

Day 1

1. Follow the steps to make another Monthly Reading Form for a sibling, cousin or friend.

2. Print it out.

3. Give it to that person and make them happy!

Lesson Review:

1. What can a spreadsheet be used for?

   ____

2. How many columns can you have in a worksheet?

   ____

3. How many rows can you have in a worksheet?

   ____

Planning for our next lesson:

1. **What is the title of your favorite book?**

   Book Title: ______________________________

2. **Tell about your favorite scene in that book:** (What characters were in that scene? What was happening?)

   ____

   ____

3. **What colors and shapes were in the scene?**

   ____

   ____

   ____

Lesson
10

10-Drawing with the computer in Publisher

About Our Project

We are going to use Microsoft Publisher to draw a picture of **a simple scene from your favorite book**. You can use stick figures for the people in your scene to make it easier. But **NO CLIP ART is allowed**!

What you will learn

- How to use computer drawing tools
- How to draw different types of lines and shapes
- How to select & resize shapes
- How to group shapes
- How to copy and paste shapes
- How to use the Undo button

How to draw with computer

As you probably have guessed, **drawing with the computer is very different** than drawing with pencils, pens or crayons. The basic idea of picking up your drawing tool and using it is the same, but once you are done drawing with the tool, you must click on it to use it again, unlike the pencil already in your hand. One main difference, which it helpful, is that **you can copy objects you have drawn** and paste them over and over again.

There are 2 simple steps to using the drawing tools:

1. Click on the tool you want to use

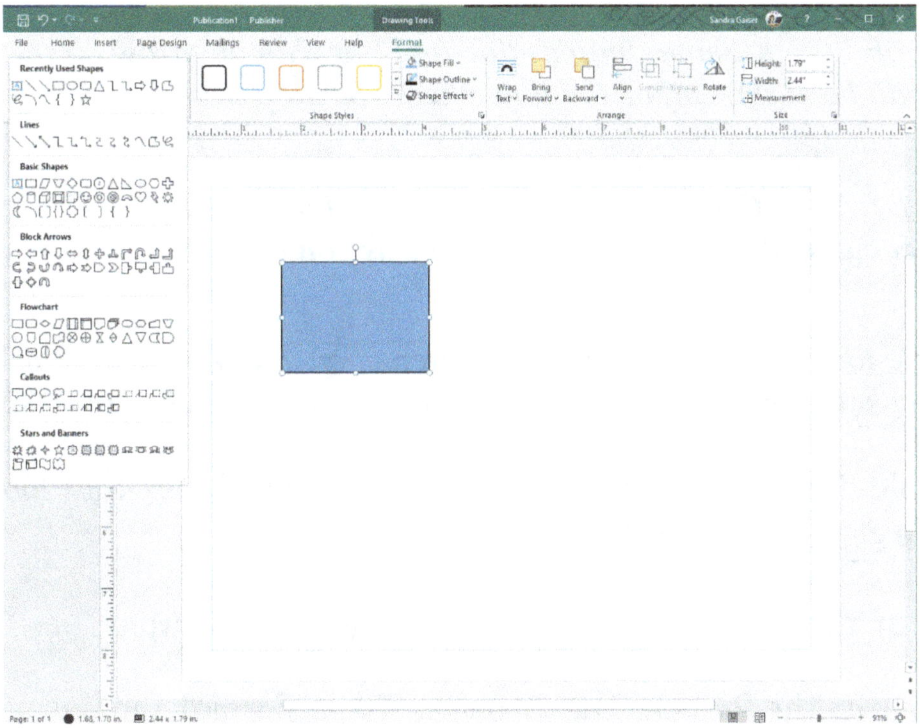

2. Click and drag with your tool to draw with it

The Drawing Tools Format tab

The **Drawing Tools Format tab** pops up on the end of the **Ribbon** when any shape is selected.

1) First, draw a shape: On the **Home** tab, in the **Objects** group, click **Shapes**.

2) Click on the shape you would like.

The Line tool: 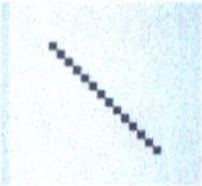 *Click this tool and click and drag the line size you want. It even automatically straightens it for you.*

The Arrow tool: 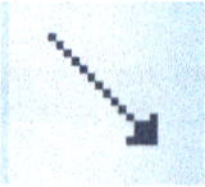 *Same thing as line tool but with an arrow on the end. The arrow point will be at the end of the line where you stop drawing.*

The Oval tool:  *Click this tool then click and drag an oval.*
Want a perfect circle? Hold down the Shift key as you drag the shape size.

The Rectangle tool:  *Click this tool then click and drag a rectangle.*
Want a perfect square? Hold down the Shift key as you drag the shape size.

3) Now hold down the mouse button and drag your mouse that looks like a big plus sign (+) across the page.

4) Let go of the mouse when the shape is the size you want.

5) Now look at the **Ribbon**. The **Drawing Tools Format** tab has popped up.

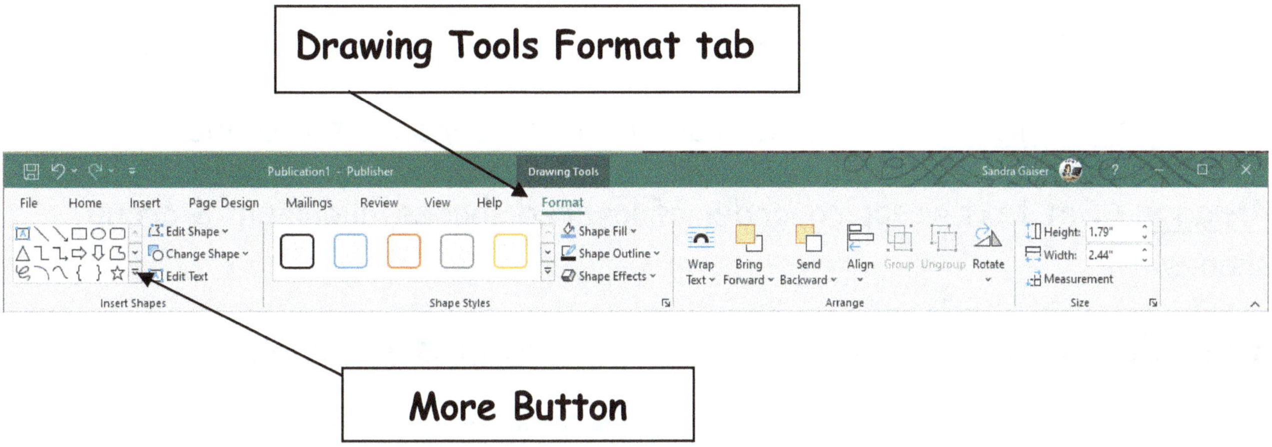

There are 4 groups on the Drawing Tools format tab:

<u>**Insert Shapes**</u> - Click on any shape, then click and drag to draw it. There are MANY more shape tools hidden under this button. Click the **More** button to see them all:

- **Lines** (double-click to stop drawing them!)
- **Connectors** (works with Flow Chart symbols for computer programmers)
- **Basic Shapes** (rectangle, octagon, cube, etc.)
- **Block Arrows**
- **Flow Chart symbols** (for computer programmers)
- **Star and Banners**
- **Call-outs:** These are great for cartoons with dialog boxes for characters

<u>**Shape Styles**</u> - Click to a preset setoff shape fill, outline and shape effects

<u>Shape Fill</u> - Click to change the fill color of any selected shape

<u>Shape Outline</u> – Click to change the outline of any selected shape

<u>Shape Effects</u> – Click to add an effect to any selected shape

<u>Arrange</u> – Set text wrapping, order of layered shapes, alignment & group shapes

<u>Size</u> – Set exact shape sizes by typing in the lengths and heights here

To add more objects to your drawing, click the Insert tab on the Ribbon. Here you can insert text boxes and WordArt:

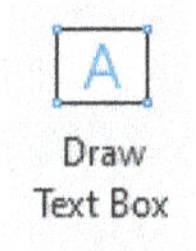

Choose the **Draw Text Box** tool: to insert words into your picture. Click and drag how big of a text box you want, and then type inside it.

Choose the **Word Art** tool: to add fancy formatted text simply and easily. Click, drag the size box you want, and then type in the words you want displayed.

Step-By-Step

Follow the steps below to create a drawing of your book scene in Publisher.

1) <u>Open Microsoft Publisher 2019:</u>
   a) In Windows 10, click the **Start** button OR in the Search box type **Publisher 2019**
   b) Click on **Publisher 2019**
2) In the top row, click on **Blank 11 x 8.5"**
3) On the **Ribbon**, on the **Home** tab, in the **Objects** group, click **Shapes**.
4) Click a shape to select it.

5) Click and hold the mouse button down and drag across the screen to draw your first shape.
6) Now the **Drawing Tools Format** tab has popped up at the end of the **Ribbon**.
7) Click on the buttons on the **Drawing Tool Format** tab to change the shape's color and style.
8) Continue adding and formatting shapes to create your drawing
9) <u>If you draw something you don't want:</u>
   a) Simply undo it by pressing CTRL-Z
   b) If you Undo too much, press CTRL-Y to Redo what you undid!
10) <u>To add color:</u>
   a) Select any **closed** shape and click the **Shape Fill** button on the **Drawing Tools Format** tab.
   b) Click on the color you want.
11) <u>Resize you shapes:</u>
   a) Click on each shape you have added to your document and using the **resize handles** (little black squares around each picture), grab the corners only and drag until the shape is the right size.
12) <u>Making copies of the shapes:</u>
   a) Select the shape
   b) Press CTRL-C for Copy
   c) Click where you want your shape
   d) Press CTRL-V to Paste
13) <u>To group the shapes:</u>
   a) Drag over the entire group of shapes to select them all
   b) Right-click and choose **Group**
   c) Now you can copy and paste the new shape

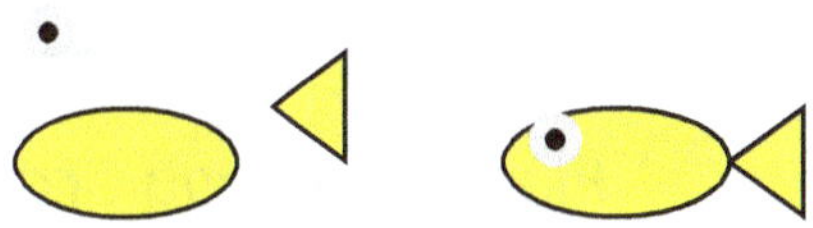

14) <u>When you have finished, print the picture:</u>
   a) Click **File**
   b) Click **Print**

c) Click **Print**

15) <u>To save the file:</u>

a) Click **File.**

b) Click **Save As**

c) Select the place where you want to save your file

d) Type in Your name and project name (example: Nick's drawing)

e) Click **Save** button.

Lesson 10 Practice

Day 1

1. **Follow the steps to make another drawing.**
2. **Print it out.**
3. **Give it to a friend!**

Lesson Review:

1. What are some shapes tools you can draw with on the computer?

____

2. How do you draw a perfect circle?

____

3. How would you draw a perfect square?

____

Planning for our next lesson:

1. **What is your favorite season of the year?**

   Favorite season: ______________________________

2. **Write down some things you would see in your favorite season.** Snowman? Rain? Fall leaves? A water skier?

   ______________ ______________ ______________

Lesson
11

11-Painting with the computer in Paint

About Our Project

We are going to use Microsoft Paint to paint a seasonal painting using a computer. Your painting should be of a scene in the summer, winter, spring or fall, for example: a snowman in a field, or some trees by a river in the fall.

What you will learn

- How to use the painting tools
- How to change the colors you paint with
- How to use the Undo button

Painting with a Computer

Again, like drawing, painting on a computer is **very different than painting on a canvas**. And again, like drawing, you still pick up the tools to use them, but this time, **you have to choose another tool or change colors in the colors palette to stop using the tool you have**. The tools are located across the top of the window on the Ribbon.

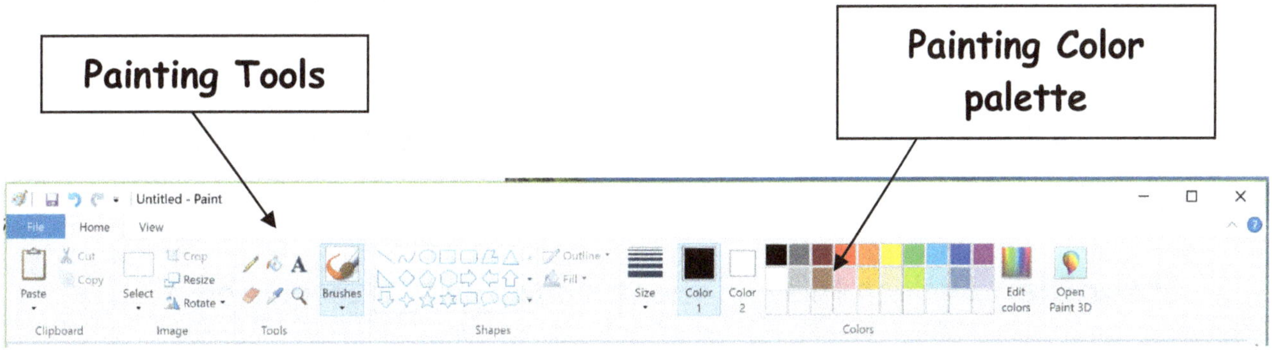

Painting Tools

Here are the painting tools and what they can be used for on the Ribbon, arrange by GROUP:

Image group:

 **Select:** Used to drag a box around multiple objects to select them.

 **Free-form select:** Use to drag over non-aligned multiple objects to select them.

Tools group:

 **Pencil:** Use this tool to draw lines like a pencil. Choose any color you like!

Fill with color: Click on this, select your color from the Color Palette, and then click on an object.

Text: Click on this tool to drag a box to type words in. Click on the color palette for font color.

Eraser: Drag over objects to erase them. Select your eraser size below the tools.

Pick color: Click on this to change the color with which you are drawing or painting.

Magnifier: Click on this and then on an object to zoom in on it.

Brushes group:

Use these tools to make wider strokes, like a paint brush. There are 9 different brushes!

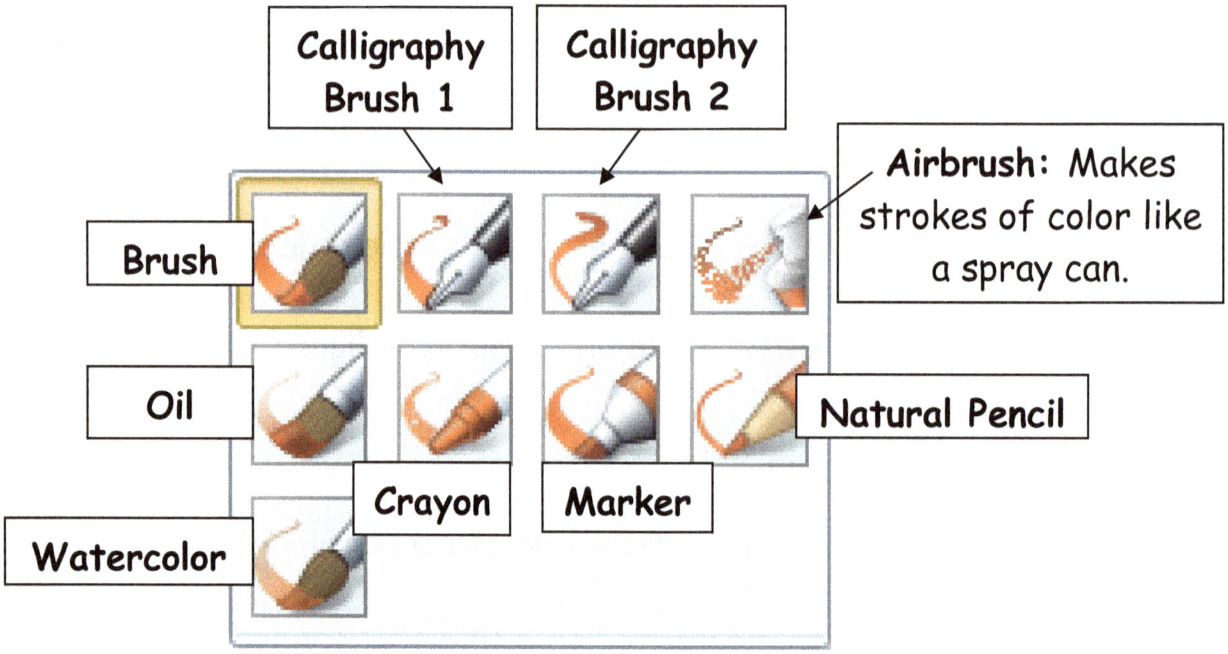

Shapes group:

Use these tool to draw different shapes, closed and un-closed.

 **Line:** Click and drag to get a line, just like the line tool in Publisher.

 **Curve:** Click and drag to get to a straight line. Then click to the side of the line to curve it.

 **Rectangle:** Click and drag to make a rectangle. Hold the Shift key down to draw a perfect square.

 **Polygon:** Use this tool to draw a many-sided figure. Click where you want the corners. Double-click to stop drawing.

 **Ellipse:** Draws an oval. To get a perfect circle, hold down the Shift key while you drag.

 **Rounded Rectangle:** Same as Rectangle tool, but this one has rounded edges.

And more! Try them all!

> Note: if you draw any CLOSED shape, it can easily be filled with color using the paint can.

Colors Palette

Click on the color that you want to draw or paint in, then click the tool you want to draw with.

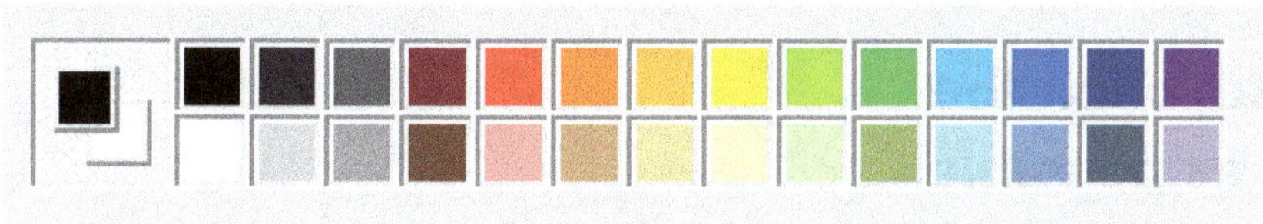

To change the colors on the color palette, click the Colors menu, then Edit Colors. Create some custom colors and add them to the palette to use.

Step-By-Step

Follow the steps below to create a painting of your own using Paint in Windows 7 or 8.

1) Open Microsoft Paint:
   a) In Windows 10, click the **Start** button OR in the Search box type **Paint**
   b) Click on **Paint**
2) Maximize your work area:
   a) Click in the upper-right hand corner on the little square to the left of the X to maximize the program window.
   b) Hover your mouse over the lower-right hand corner of the white painting canvas and drag it down close to the lower right edge of the window but can still see the page edges. This gives you the most area to paint in.
3) Begin your drawing:
   a) Pick a color and a tool and start drawing.
4) If you want a horizon line:
   a) Draw it now, all the way to the edges of the paper. This will create 2 closed rectangle shapes, one for sky and one for ground.
   b) Use the paint can to fill the sky blue and the ground white for snow, brown for dirt, green for grass, or blue for water.

If you make a mistake, click the Undo button as soon as possible.

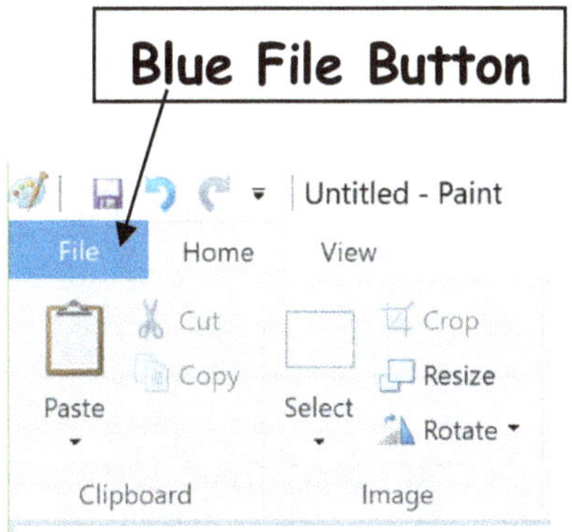

5) When you have finished, print the painting:
   a) Click the **blue File button**
   b) Click **Print**
   c) Click **Print**

6) To save the file:
   a) Click the **blue File button**
   b) Click **Save As**
   c) Type in Your name and project name (example: Nick's painting)
   d) Click **Save** button.

Lesson 11 Practice

Day 1

1. **Follow the steps to make another painting of a season.**
2. **Print it out.**
3. **Give it to a friend!**

Lesson Review:

1. Name 3 brushes you can paint with on the computer.

   ____

2. Name 3 of the shapes you can paint with on the computer.

   ____

3. Name 3 tools you can paint with on the computer.

   ____

Planning for our next lesson:

1. **For whom will you make a Thanksgiving card?**

   ____

2. **Write down some things you would like to put on your Thanksgiving card:**

   ____________ ____________ ____________

Lesson

12

12-Making a Thanksgiving Card in Publisher

About Our Project

We are going to use Microsoft Publisher to make a Thanksgiving card. Choose someone for which to make the card: grandparents, aunt, uncle, or parents.

What you will learn

- How to use a greeting card template
- How to change the layout of a greeting card
- How to change the color scheme
- How to change the font scheme
- How to change the verse
- Learn how to change the card size

Greeting Card Templates

Microsoft Publisher has the ability to make all kinds of greeting cards quickly. Many **templates** are included for **holidays and special occasions**. You **can use the cards the way they are** or **change any part of them** including the words, colors, pictures and styles. The templates are:

- Birthday
- Holiday (Christmas, Easter, Halloween, Hanukkah, New Year's, Ramadan, Rosh Hashanah, St. Patrick's Day, Thanksgiving, Mother's Day, Father's Day, Grandparent's Day, Kwanzaa, Valentine's Day, & Bat Mitzvah)
- Gift Card
- Thank You
- Anniversary
- Note
- Graduation
- Wedding
- New baby
- New home
- Retirement
- Friendship
- Romance
- I'm sorry
- Get well
- Sympathy
- Good luck
- We've moved
- Engagement
- Birth announcement
- Reminder

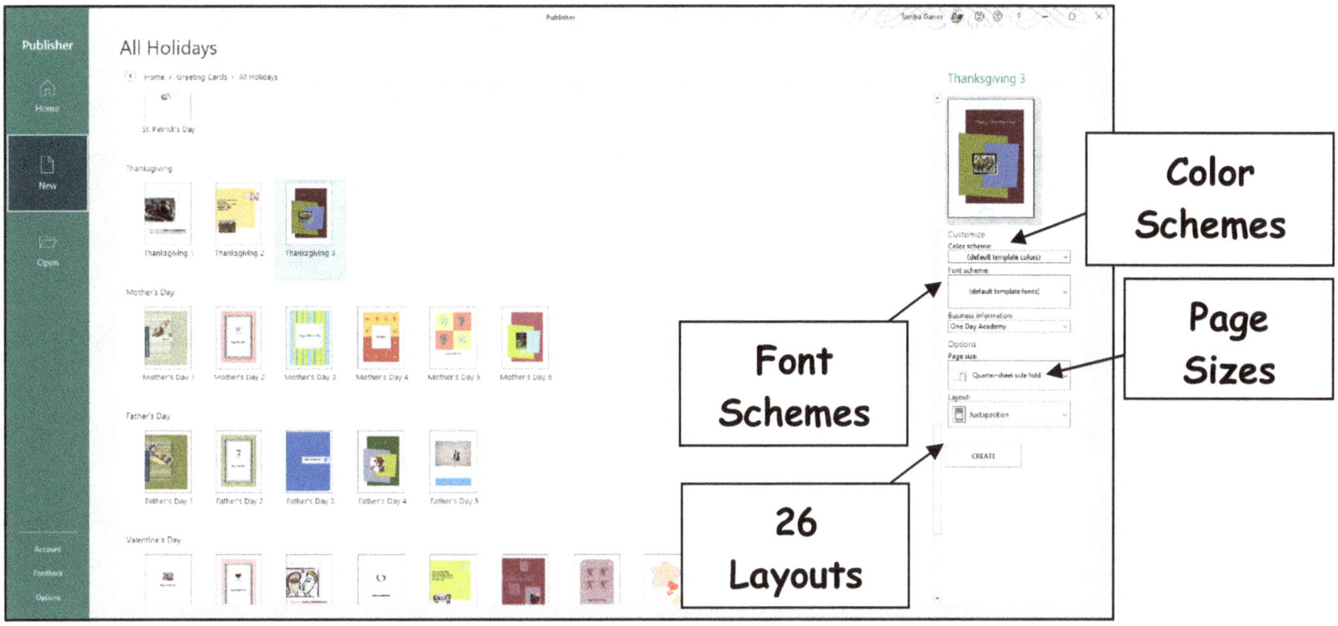

Greeting Card Layouts

There are **26 different greeting card layouts** to choose from. Each one mixes up the graphics and text boxes on the card with different styles and colors. Try each one and **you pick the one you like the best**!

Color Schemes

Once you choose the **Layout** that you like, you can change the **Color Scheme** either in that window OR later using the **Page Design** tab on the **Ribbon**. Simply hover your mouse over each scheme and see it previewed on your card. Click on the one you like the best!

Font Schemes

You can also change the **Font Scheme** either in that window OR later on using the **Page Design** tab on the **Ribbon**. Simply hover your mouse over each scheme and see it previewed on your card. Click on the one you like the best!

Page Size

Publisher gives you options to print the card either a **quarter-page size** to fit in an invitation-sized envelope or a **half-page size** which is more like a store-bought card.

Step-By-Step

Follow the steps below to create a Thanksgiving Card.

1) Open Microsoft Publisher 2019:
   a) In Windows 10, click the **Start** button OR in the Search box type **Publisher 2019**
   b) Click on **Publisher 2019**
2) Open a pre-designed Thanksgiving Card template:
   a) Click **BUILT-IN**
   b) Click on **Greeting Cards**
   c) In the **Holidays** row, click at the far right-end on the yellow folder **All Holidays**
   d) Scroll down several rows, alphabetically, to the **Thanksgiving** row with 3 card templates.
   e) Click **ONCE** on the Thanksgiving Card style that you like (don't double-click or you will go right into the publication before you can choose your options)

Remember: You can change the Layout, Color Scheme & Fonts! The only difference between the cards is the pictures.

3) In the right task pane, **Customize** the card the way you want it:

a) <u>Change the Color scheme</u>
   i) Click **Color Scheme** on right side
   ii) Click a color scheme you like. Try as many as you like, only the last choice stays.

b) <u>Change the Font scheme</u>
   i) Click **Font Scheme** on right side
   ii) Click a font scheme you like. Try as many as you like, only the last choice stays.

c) <u>Change the Page Size of the Card:</u>
   i) Choose quarter-fold (prints on one side of page) or half-fold (prints on both sides of page)

d) <u>Change the Layout of the Card:</u>
   i) Choose one of 26 different layouts under **Layout** (lower right corner), click the little arrow
   ii) Try different **Layouts** until you find the right one for you

e) Click **Create** at the bottom when you're done

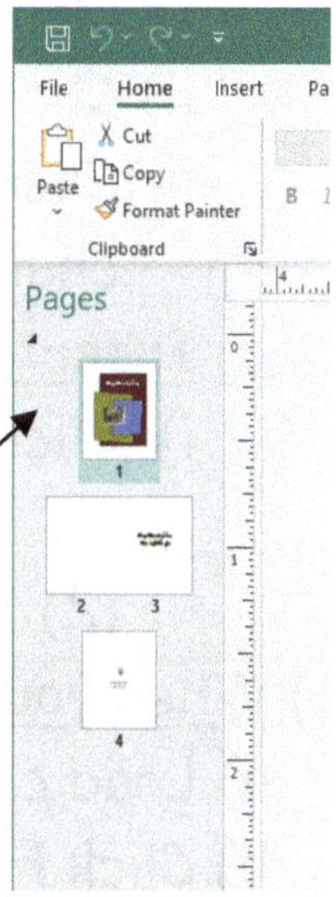

4) <u>To change sides of the card:</u>
   a) In the **Pages Pane** on the left side of the window, click the side of the card you want to edit.

5) <u>Customize the greeting card the way you want it:</u>
   a) <u>Change the built-in verse options:</u>
      i) Click the **Page Design** tab on the **Ribbon**
      ii) In the **Template** group, click the **Options** button

      iii) Click on the **Available Messages** on the left column to

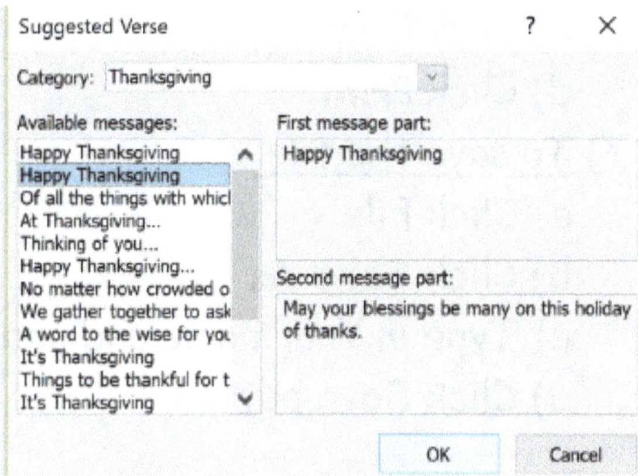

see what they say in the right column

iv) Click **OK** when you have chosen the one you want

OR You can type and change the words on all 4 sides of the card

---

b) Change the color scheme
   i) On the **Ribbon**, click the **Page Design** tab
   ii) Click on the colors you like. Try as many as you like, only the last choice stays.

c) Change the font scheme
   i) On the **Ribbon**, click the **Page Design** tab
   ii) Click **Fonts**
   iii) Click a font scheme you like. Try as many as you like, only the last choice stays.

d) Insert online pictures or your own pictures
   i) Click **Insert**
      (1) Click **Pictures,** to use a photo you have taken
      (2) Or click **Online Pictures**

6) When you have finished, print the greeting card:
   a) Load card stock in the printer
   b) Click **File**
   c) Click **Print**
   d) Click **Print**

7) To save the file:
   a) Click **File**
   b) Click **Save As**
   c) Type in Your name and project name (example: Nick's greeting card)
   d) Click **Save** button.

Lesson 12 Practice

Day 1

1. Follow the steps to make another greeting card for someone else.

2. Print it out.

3. Give it to them!

Lesson Review:

1. Name 3 other greeting cards you can make in Publisher.

   ____

2. How many different greeting card layouts are there?

   ____

3. Which page size fits an invitation-size envelope?

   ____

Planning for our next lesson:

1. **Who will you be giving Christmas gifts to this year?**

2. **What gifts will you make or buy for each one?**

Lesson 13

13-Make a Christmas Gift Budget in Excel

A nice form to keep track of all the wonderful gifts you will give this year!

About Our Project

We are going to make a gift budget in Excel to keep track of the gifts we want to give to people for Christmas this year and the money we spend on them. It can be a real budget based on a real amount of money you have to spend, or you can have an imaginary budget with as much money as you want!

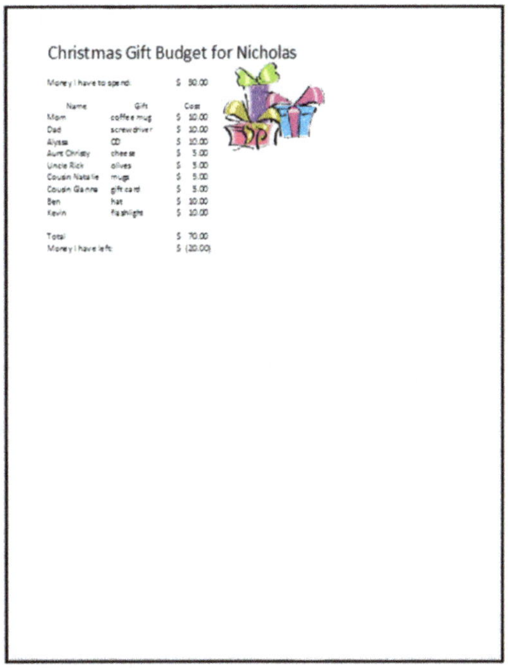

Christmas Gift Budget for Nicholas

Money I have to spend:		$ 50.00
Name	Gift	Cost
Mom	coffee mug	$ 10.00
Dad	screwdriver	$ 10.00
Alyssa	CD	$ 10.00
Aunt Christy	cheese	$ 5.00
Uncle Rick	olives	$ 5.00
Cousin Natalie	mugs	$ 5.00
Cousin Gianna	gift card	$ 5.00
Ben	hat	$ 10.00
Kevin	flashlight	$ 10.00
Total		$ 70.00
Money I have left:		$ (20.00)

What you will learn

- What a gift budget is
- How to add & subtract in Excel
- How to write a formula in Excel
- How to use a function in Excel

A Gift Budget

__A budget is:__ a list of estimated income and expenditures for a given time-period or event

We are going to make a gift budget. In other words, we will list the amount of money we will have to **SPEND** on gifts this year (our income). Then, we will subtract how much each gift will **COST** (our expenditures). If the final total is zero, we will have spent all the money we have.

Christmas Gift Budget for Nicholas

Money I have to spend:		$ 50.00
Name	Gift	Cost
Mom	coffee mug	$ 10.00
Dad	screwdriver	$ 10.00
Alyssa	CD	$ 10.00
Aunt Christy	cheese	$ 5.00
Uncle Rick	olives	$ 5.00
Cousin Natalie	mugs	$ 5.00
Cousin Gianna	gift card	$ 5.00
Ben	hat	$ 10.00
Kevin	flashlight	$ 10.00
Total		$ 70.00
Money I have left:		$ (20.00)

Let's get started!

A formula in Excel

A formula in Excel is the same as any mathematical formula:

3 + 4 = 7   or   7 - 4 = 3

except we type them in differently in Excel. To make sure Excel knows we want to calculate we **start with an equal sign** and then type the rest of the formula:

=3+4   **or**   **=7-4**   (and NO spaces)

Then when you press Enter, you will see the result of your calculation in the cell, instead of your formula.

Also, Excel is smart enough to not only add up numbers you type in, but it **can grab numbers** from inside a cell and work with those as well. You just must tell it where to look! This way, **if the numbers in the cells change, then the answer to the formula will to**!

Instead of **=34+79+68+90**   use   **=B2+B3+B4+B5**

Finding a cell

Remember, Excel is like the game Battleship®, you locate a cell by its column letter + row number: **B4** would be the cell where column B and row 4 cross.

NOW IT'S YOUR TURN...

---

1. Put your right pointer finger on the screen at the top of the B column.
2. Now, put your left index finger at the front of the 4th row.

3. Now slide your right finger DOWN and your left finger ACROSS at the same time till your fingers touch.
4. Cell **B4**! You found it!

A function in Excel

A function in Excel is **a prewritten formula** that takes a value or values, performs an operation, and returns a new value or values. Use functions to simplify and shorten formulas on a worksheet, especially those that perform long or difficult calculations. For example, instead of adding up many cells in a worksheet one by one, simply use the SUM function:

Instead of **=A4+B4+C4+D4+E4+F4+G4** use **=SUM(A4:G4)**

A formula starts after the = sign and is a special word that will perform a special math task:

- **SUM** will add up all the numbers listed in the function
- **AVERAGE** will add up all the numbers and then divide by the number of numbers
- **MIN** will give the smallest number in the list of numbers in the formula
- **MAX** will give the largest number in the list of numbers in the formula

There is a button on the Ribbon for the SUM function because it is used so much, called **AutoSum**. Its symbol is the Greek letter Sigma Σ. The little arrow next to it will also do the other functions above.

Step-By-Step

Follow the steps below to create a Christmas Gift Budget.

1) <u>Open Microsoft Excel 2019:</u>
   a) In Windows 10, click the **Start** button OR in the Search box type **Excel 2019**
   b) Click on **Excel 2019**
2) <u>Click **Blank Workbook**</u>
3) <u>Title the gift budget:</u>
   a) In cell A1 type **Christmas Gift Budget for (type your name)**
   b) Press **Enter**
4) <u>Now let's enter the column headings:</u>
   a) Click on cell A3 and type **Money I Have to Spend:**

Don't worry that the words in cell A3 got cut off. We will fix that!

   b) Press **TAB** twice on your keyboard to move to cell C3.
   c) Type the amount of money you have (or would love to have!) to spend. Just type the numbers; we'll add the dollar signs later.
   d) Press **Enter**.
   e) Click on cell A5. Type **Name**.
   f) Press **TAB** to move to cell B5. Type **Gift**.
   g) Press **TAB** to move to cell C5. Type **Cost**.
   h) Press **TAB**.
5) <u>Now, to widen the columns:</u>
   a) Hover your mouse between the column heading letters A and B. You should see a two-headed black arrow. Click and drag to the right until it is 230 pixels wide.

If you double-click, the column will automatically resize to the widest item – here, it's our title.

- b) Hover your mouse between the column heading letters B and C. You should see a two-headed black arrow. Click and drag to the right until it is 300 pixels wide.

6) Let's add dollar signs:
   - a) Click on the column heading for column **C** (click right on it) to select the whole column.
   - b) Click the **$** on the **Ribbon**, on the **Home** tab in the **Number** group.

7) Let's center the column headings:
   - a) Click right on the row number 5 to select the whole row.
   - b) Click the **Center** button on the **Ribbon** in the **Alignment Group**.
   - c) Click the **B** in the **Font** group to make them Bold.

8) Now, to enter the names, gifts and cost of each gift:
   - a) Click on cell A6 and type name of the 1st person you a getting a Christmas gift and press **TAB**.
   - b) Now type in the name of the gift you would like to get or make the person and press **TAB**.
   - c) Now type in the approximate cost of the gift (don't forget to add the tax!).
   - d) Keep typing in names, gifts and costs until finished.

9) Now to find out how much money we have spent:
   - a) In column A, 2 lines below the final name on your list, type the word **Total**.
   - b) Press **TAB** twice to column C.
   - c) Click the Σ AutoSum button on the **Ribbon**, on the **Home** tab in the **Editing** Group.
   - d) Press **Enter**. Excel added up all the costs for you!

10) Now take a look in Print Preview

a) Click **File**, then **Print**.

b) Click ⓒ to get out of Print Preview.

11) Now to create a Formula to see how much money we have left in our budget:

a) Click in the cell below **Total**.

b) Type **Money I have left:**

c) Press **TAB** twice.

d) Type an =, then click on C3, then type a hyphen -, then click on the total costs cell.

e) Press **Enter**.

f) If the number you get is in parentheses ($20.00), you spent too much. Lower some of the numbers until the ( ) go away. Now you should have spent just what you have to spend (or a little less!).

12) Now to make the title nicer:

a) Click on A1.

b) Change the font style and size (22 is a good title size font).

13) Insert a picture of a Christmas gift in the upper right corner:

a) Click the **Insert** tab

b) Click **Online Pictures**.

c) Search for the word **Christmas**.

d) Click on the picture that you like.

e) Click **Insert**.

f) Drag it up to the top of the form.

14) When you have finished, print the form:

a) Click **File**

b) Click **Print**

c) Click **Print**

15) To save the file:

a) Click **File**

b) Click **Save As**

c) Choose where you want to save your file
d) Type in Your name and project name (example: Nick's Gift Budget)
e) Click **Save** button

Lesson 13 Practice

Day 1

1. Follow the steps to make another budget for spending and saving your allowance.

2. Print it out.

Lesson Review:

1. Give an example of a formula in Excel:

____

2. Give an example of a function in Excel:

____

3. What is a budget?

____

Planning for our next lesson:

1. **If you have no money to spend on gifts, you can always MAKE your gifts. Who would you like to make gifts for this year?**

   ________________ ________________ ________________

   ________________ ________________ ________________

2. **What meal can you plan or cook for your family?**

   ____

3. **What things do you like to do for your family? (Make meals, clean the house, wash the car, etc.?**

   ________________ ________________ ________________

   ________________ ________________ ________________

4. **What ideas do you have for some gifts you could make with the computer?**

   ________________ ________________ ________________

   ________________ ________________ ________________

   ________________ ________________ ________________

Lesson

14

14-Make Printable Gifts in Publisher

Fun ways to give from your heart with things you can do for others!

About Our Project

Did you know you can make gifts in Publisher that can be customized and printed on any printer? You can choose from gift certificates menus, gift card holders, or calendars.

What you will learn

- What a printable gift can be
- How to use a gift certificate template
- How to use a menu template
- How to change print formats

What are printable gifts?

A printable gift is a gift that you can print out on your printer right after you create it. They work great for:

- gifts from the heart
- gifts of your time or talents
- last minute gifts
- gifts only you can give

It could be a gift certificate for:

- a **hand car wash**
- to **walk someone's dog**
- or for **a hug**

It could be a menu for:

- **a special meal** that you can cook
- or just set up

Whatever you choose, be sure to use **plenty of imagination** to think up your custom-made gifts!

Gift certificates

Step-By-Step

Follow the steps below to create gift certificates.

1) <u>Open Microsoft Publisher 2019:</u>
   a) In Windows 10, click the **Start** button OR in the Search box type **Publisher 2019**
   b) Click on **Publisher 2019**
2) <u>Choose your gift certificate template & design it:</u>
   e) From the **Publisher 2019** opening screen, click **BUILT-IN**
   a) Choose ***Gift Certificates***

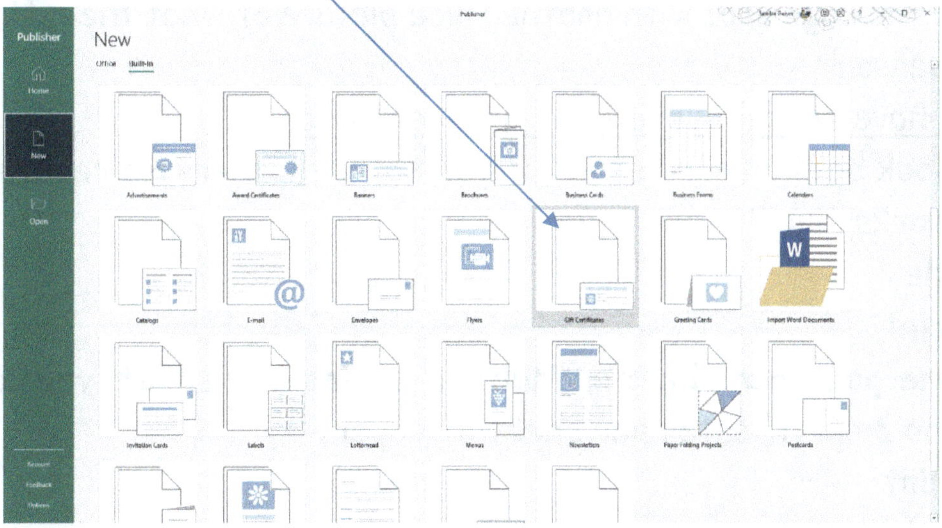

   b) Then click **ONCE** on the style you like (don't double-click or you will go right into the publication before you can choose your options)
   c) Customize it using the options in the right-hand task pane:
      i) Choose the color scheme (**Mistletoe** works well for Christmas gift certificates)
      ii) Choose the font scheme (fancy styles work well here)
   d) Then click ***Create*** at the bottom.

3) Now, customize it:
   a) You can type in the recipient's name after **This certificate entitles:** or leave it blank to hand write name in after you print it.
   b) After the **To:**, you can type in what your gift is: car wash, house cleaning, homemade cookies, etc. Again, you can leave this blank if you wish to hand write this after printing.
   c) **Authorized by:** means you! Type your name here.
   d) Choose an expiration date (the date they can't use the certificate anymore) and type it after **Expires:**. It can also say *Never Expires.*
   e) Enter the **Number:** of the certificate or just make one up!
   f) Your address should only be on it for close friends and family to see. Otherwise, just delete that text box and replace it with a nice picture.
   g) Replace the **Logo** spot with another nice picture of what the gift is or of the season!
4) When you have finished, print the gift certificate:
   a) These look best on card stock, if you have it, otherwise regular paper works fine.
   b) Click **File**
   c) Click **Print**
   d) Click **One page per sheet** or **Multiple copies per sheet** (you can have 1 or 3 certificates per sheet of paper)
   e) Click **Print**
5) To save the file:
   a) Click **File**
   b) Click **Save As**
   c) Choose where you want to save your file
   d) Type in Your name and project name (example: Nick's Gift certificates).
   e) Click **Save** button

Custom-made menus

Christmas Breakfast Menu

By Alyssa and Nick

Christmas Day 2016

Cinnamon Rolls A brief description of the dish.	FREE
Fresh Fruit Apples, oranges & grapes	FREE
Eggs Any way you like	FREE
Bacon Crispy or soggy	FREE
Orange juice Freshly squeezed	FREE

MERRY CHRISTMAS

Step-By-Step

Follow the steps below to create a custom menu.

1) Open Microsoft Publisher 2019:
   a) In Windows 10, click the **Start** button OR in the Search box type **Publisher 2019**
   b) Click on **Publisher 2019**
2) Choose your menu template & design it:
   a) From the **Publisher 2019** opening screen, click **BUILT-IN**
   b) Choose **Menus**

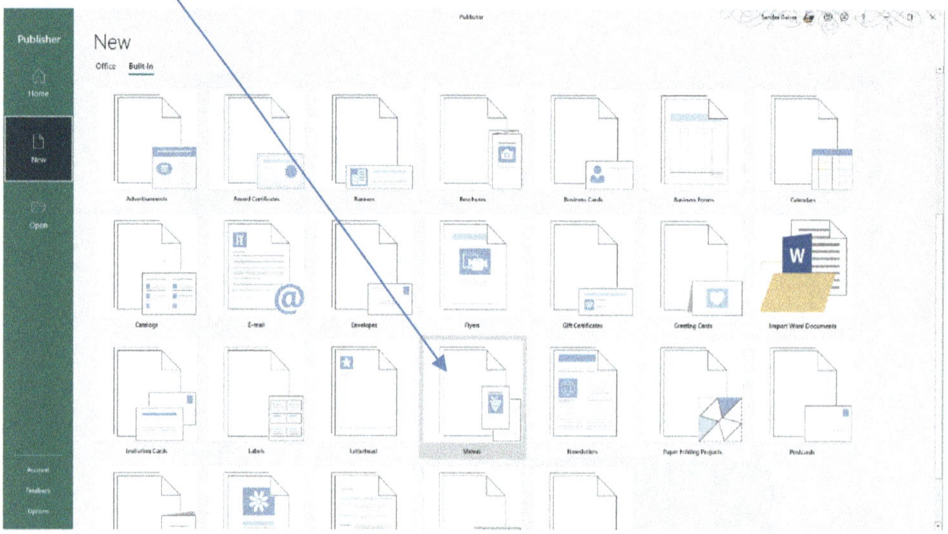

   c) Then **click ONCE** on the style you like (don't double-click or you will go right into the publication before you can choose your options)

For a short menu, a Daily Special or a Wine/Dessert menu style works best because they print on 1 side of the page & you can print 1 big copy or 4 little copies per page.

The Regular & Take-Out menu styles hold 6-sides of information and prints on both sides of the page. These work best for real restaurants.

3) Customize it using the options in the right-hand task pane:
   a) Choose the color scheme (**Mistletoe** works well for Christmas menus)
   b) Choose the font scheme (fancy styles work well here)
   c) Choose the page size:
      i) **Quarter-page** to print small menus, 1 or 4 per page (great for a meal for a family)
      ii) **Full-page** to print 1 large menu that fills the whole page
   d) Then click **Create** at the bottom.
4) Now, fill in the menu with your meal information:
   a) Replace **Business Name** with a pretend name of your restaurant or the event you are celebrating
   b) Add the kind of menu you are making: breakfast, lunch, dinner, or dessert
   c) Enter in the "Date" of your special meal, if you know it, or put "Whenever you choose"
   d) Enter the menu items
   e) Enter descriptions of the menu items
   f) Add prices if you like. Or put FREE. Or just delete the price.
   g) Replace the Logo spot with a nice picture of the meal or the season
   h) At the bottom, type a nice, little message to your diners.
5) When you have finished, print the menu:
   a) These look best on card stock, if you have it, otherwise regular paper works fine.
   b) Click **File**
   c) Click **Print**

MAKE SURE TO FOLLOW YOUR PRINTER'S INSTRUCTIONS to print double-sided.

For Regular & Take-Out menus (1 per sheet & prints on both sides of the paper):

i) Click **Print** to print first side
ii) Then flip paper to print the other side of the menu.
iii) Fold to make a tri-fold menu

For Daily Special or Wine/Dessert menus (1 or 4 copies per sheet):

i) Click **One page per sheet** or **Multiple copies per sheet** (you can have 1 or 4 per sheet)
ii) Click **Print**

5) To save the file:
   a) Click **File**
   b) Click **Save As**
   c) Type in Your name and project name (example: Nick's Gift certificates).
   d) Click **Save** button

Lesson 14 Practice

Day 1

1. Follow the steps to make more printable gifts for friends and family.

2. Print them out.

3. Give them away!

Lesson Review:

1. How many gift certificates can you print on one sheet of paper?

____

2. Name one menu that prints on BOTH sides of the paper?

____

3. How many Daily Special menus can fit on one page?

____

Planning for our next lesson:

1. **To whom will you be writing thank you cards this year?**

____________ ____________ ____________

____________ ____________ ____________

____________ ____________ ____________

Lesson

15

15-Thank You Postcards in Publisher

A nice way to say "Thank you!" for the wonderful gifts you receive!

About Our Project

Now when the holidays are over, you probably need to write some thank you cards. Postcards are a quick and simple way to thank all your friends and family.

What you will learn

- How to use a postcard template in Publisher
- How to print on both sides of the publication

Postcards

A postcard is a neat combination of a letter and an envelope. There's enough room on one side to write a little note. The other side you address just like an envelope: recipient's address in the middle, your return address in the upper left-hand corner, and the stamp goes in the upper right-hand corner.

Postcards must be printed on card stock because they are mailed without an envelope. The nice thing about that is it costs less postage to mail them because they are lighter. Be sure to ask the Post Office for the cheaper stamps to mail these.

Postcards must be printed on both sides. Make sure you know how your specific printer does this. If you are not sure, read the documentation that came with your printer.

We will design a basic postcard that prints out 4 at a time. Then you can just cut them out, fill them in for each specific gift, affix stamps and mail them!

Step-By-Step

Follow the steps below to create holiday thank you postcards.

1) Open Microsoft Publisher 2019:
   a) In Windows 10, click the **Start** button OR in the Search box type **Publisher 2019**
   b) Click on **Publisher 2019**
2) Open a pre-designed holiday postcard template:
   a) Click **BUILT-IN**
   b) Click on **Postcards**
   c) In the **Marketing** row, click at the far right-end on the yellow folder ***All Marketing***
   d) Scroll down several rows to the **Holiday Thank You** row with 3 postcard templates.

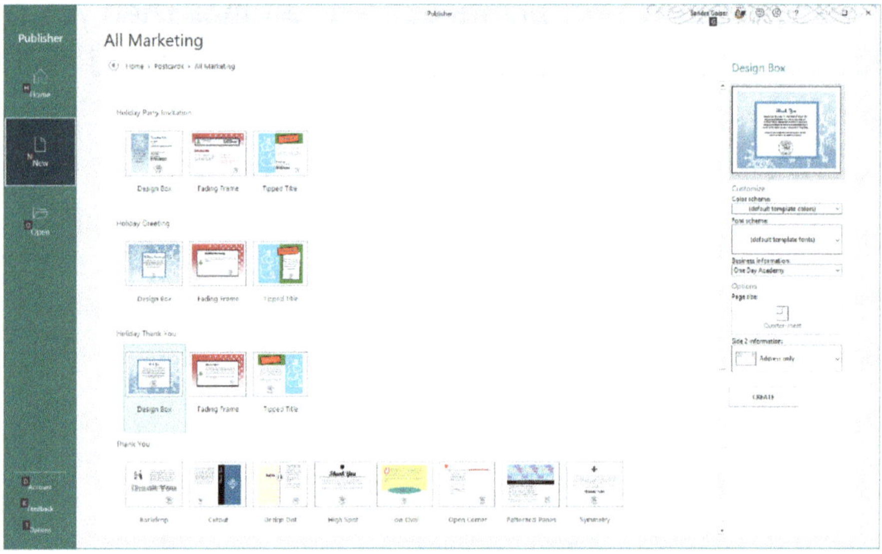

   e) Click **ONCE** on the **Holiday Postcard Thank You** style that you like (don't double-click or you will go right into the publication before you can choose your options)

f) You can customize it using the options in the right-hand task pane:
   i) Choose a **Color scheme** (if you don't like the default one)
   ii) Choose a **Font scheme**
   iii) The **Page size** is already set to **Quarter-sheet**
   iv) Set the **Side 2 information** to **Address only**

g) Click **Create** at the bottom.

3) Now, make the card ready to hand write on:

Since you will print 4 identical postcards, and you won't need 4 cards thanking Grandma for that scarf she gave you, we will put blank lines to be written on after printing.

a) Delete all the text out of the middle area.

b) Add blank lines by holding down the **underscore key** (Shift-dash).

c) Press **Enter** when a line is all the way across the card. *This puts a wider space between the lines so it's easier to write on with a pen or pencil.*

d) Click on pyramid & delete the **Organization** logo, then insert a nice holiday picture.

4) Make lines for the Recipient's Address on the other side of the card:

a) Flip the card over: In the **Pages Pane** on the left side of the window, click on the **2** to see the other side of the postcard.

b) Delete the text inside the middle box.

c) Hold down the **Underscore key** until it reaches the end of the line.

d) Press **Enter** 2 times (this makes even wider spaces between the lines). You will only need 3 lines.

5) Type your Return Address on the card:

a) In the upper-right corner, delete the **Business Name** box and move the **Primary Business Address** box up to the blue line.

Make sure you click the EDGE OF THE BOXES to select the entire box before deleting or moving the text boxes.

b) Type your own address in the box for the **Return Address**. It will print the same on all 4 postcards. (Or delete that box & use your return address labels we made in class!)

c) You can add a small picture ONLY on the left side of the recipient's address. The rest of the postcard should be left blank.

6) When you have finished, print the postcards:

a) Insert only 1 sheet of card stock in your printer.

These must be printed on card stock, or you can't mail them.

b) Click **File**
c) Click **Print**
d) Click **Multiple copies per sheet**
e) Make sure the **Orientation** is **Landscape** (you should see 4 postcard fronts)
f) Click **Print** to print side 1
g) **CAREFULLY** place the printed sheet back into the paper feed **ACCORDING TO YOUR PRINTER'S** directions
h) Press the print button on your printer to print side 2

7) To save the file:
   a) Click **File**
   b) Click **Save As**
   c) Type in Your name and project name (example: Nick's thank you postcards).
   d) Click **Save** button

8) Use the postcards:
   a) Cut the 4 postcards apart
   b) Fill them out
   c) Put a postcard postage stamp on each one
   d) Mail them!

Lesson 15 Practice

Day 1

1. Follow the steps to make more thank you postcards to use throughout the year.

2. Print them out.

Lesson Review:

1. What is a postcard?

   ____

2. Do postcards need more or less postage than a letter in an envelope?

   ____

3. Are postcards printed on both sides of the paper?

   ____

Planning for our next lesson:

1. **Think about what kind of photo you would like to put on a calendar you will make for someone:**

Grandparents and relatives would like a calendar with a picture of you on it.
Siblings might like a photo of their favorite sport or hobby.
If your family owns a business, you could use the business logo or products you sell.

Who will you make your photo calendar for: ____________________

2. **Either take a photo or copy a photo onto your computer or flash drive to have ready for class next time.** Or you can use a photo we take in class of you.

3. **You may use more than one photo if you like on your calendar.**

Lesson 16

16-Make a Photo Calendar in Publisher

A nice gift for friends and family, and you can use any photo you want!

About Our Project

We are going to make another gift that can be used for the New Year. It's a yearly calendar with any photo you like added to it. Be sure to pick a photo that the person you are giving it to would like.

What you will learn

- How to use photo calendar templates in Publisher
- How to edit a photo in Publisher

A Yearly Calendar

Many people need a yearly calendar to see the whole year on a single page for long-term scheduling. **You can also make monthly calendars**, too, just by changing the Timeframe setting. It's your choice, but if you choose the monthly timeframe, you will have to print all 12 pages for the person as a gift. For today, let's try just the yearly calendar on a single page.

Editing Photos

It's easy to edit photos and pictures while you are in any Microsoft Office application. Just click on the photo or picture and **Picture Tools Format** contextual tab will be added to the **Ribbon** at the right end of it. Click it and you can make all kinds of editing choices.

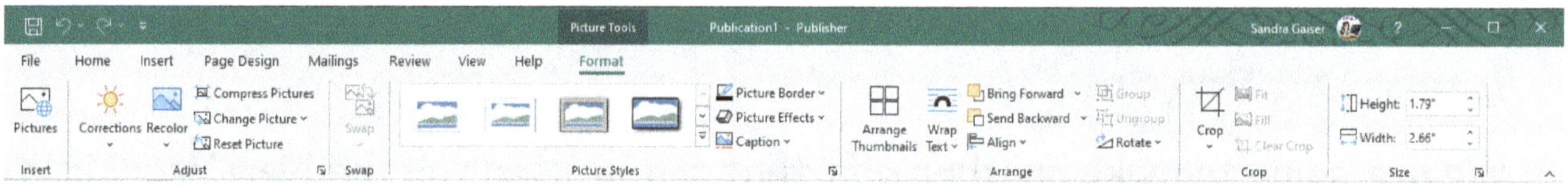

Insert: Use this to insert a photo of your own

Adjust:
- Use this to adjust brightness & contrast of photos
- Recolor pictures
- Compress pictures so they take up less disk space in the document the are in
- Change picture to a new one that fits where the old picture was
- Reset picture to its original settings

Swap: Swaps 2 photo positions

Picture Styles:
- Use this to quickly style pictures using pre-set choices
- Set border choices
- Change picture shape
- Add a caption

Arrange:
- Change photo layering
- Align pictures
- Group pictures or objects together
- Rotate pictures or objects

Crop: Use this to cut off parts of your photos you don't want

Size: Sets size

Step-By-Step

Follow the steps below to create a yearly photo calendar.

1) Open Microsoft Publisher 2019:
   a) In Windows 10, click the **Start** button OR in the Search box type **Publisher 2019**
   b) Click on **Publisher 2019**
2) Open a pre-designed Photo Calendar template:
   a) Click **BUILT-IN**
   b) Click on **Calendars**

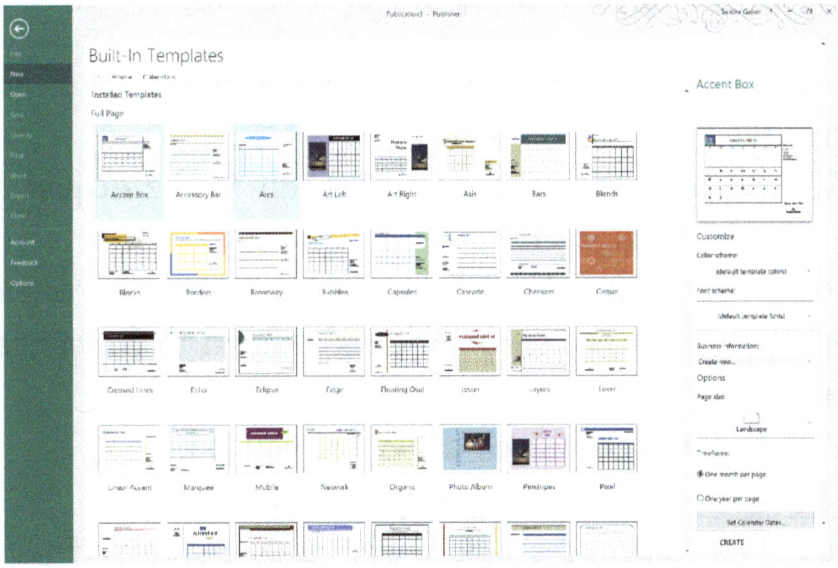

You can choose any calendar with a big photo on it (Art Left, Art Right, Photo Album, Pinstripes, Travel or Varsity styles)

   c) Then **click ONCE** on the style you like (don't double-click or you will go right into the publication before you can choose your options)
   d) Customize it using the options in the right-hand task pane:

i) Choose a **Color scheme**
ii) Choose a **Font scheme**
iii) Choose the **Page size**: portrait or landscape
iv) Be sure to set the Timeframe to • One year per page
v) Click **Set Calendar Dates** to set the start date and end date to next year

e) Then click **Create** at the bottom.

3) Now, change the picture(s):

Choose or take a photo of something or someone that you think the person would like to see on their calendar: you, a family, a favorite animal or sport, a landscape, etc.

a) Make sure the photo is on your computer or on a device connected to your computer.
b) Click the existing photo, on the **Format** tab, in the **Adjust** group, choose **Change Picture**, **Change Picture**.
c) Navigate to where your photo is located or search for one online.
d) Double-click it. It will be automatically resized to fit where the other picture was.
e) You can also insert some small clip art if you like.

4) When you have finished, print the calendar:
a) These look best on card stock. Insert only 1 sheet of card stock in your printer.
b) Click **File**
c) Click **Print**, then **Print**

5) To save the file:
a) Click **File**
b) Click **Save As**
c) Type in Your name and project name (example: Nick's calendar).
d) Click **Save** button

Lesson 16 Practice

Day 1

1. Follow the steps to make another calendar for a friend or a relative.

2. Print it out.

3. Give it!

Lesson Review:

1. What does the CROP button do?

____

2. Can you print a MONTHLY calendar?

____

3. How would you change the BRIGHTNESS of your photo?

____

Planning for our next lesson:

1. **What is your favorite animal?** ______________________

2. **Write down 3 things that make that animal different from other animals.** Color? Furry? Mammal? Cold-blooded?

______________ ______________ ______________

Lesson

17

17-Creating an Outline in Word

An easy way to organize your thoughts before writing an essay or research paper!

About Our Project

Outlines are a great way to organize your thoughts before you write an essay, a research paper, prepare a presentation or do a project. Let's make an outline about your favorite animal.

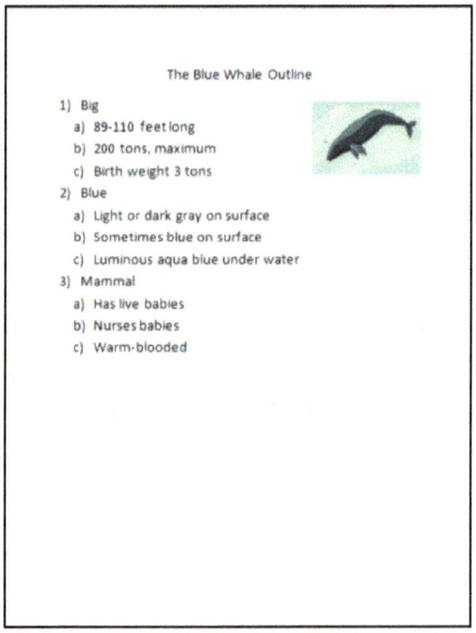
The Blue Whale Outline

1) Big
   a) 89-110 feet long
   b) 200 tons, maximum
   c) Birth weight 3 tons
2) Blue
   a) Light or dark gray on surface
   b) Sometimes blue on surface
   c) Luminous aqua blue under water
3) Mammal
   a) Has live babies
   b) Nurses babies
   c) Warm-blooded

What you will learn

- What an outline is
- Outline styles
- How to make an outline in Word
- How to use outline view in Word
- How to promote & demote outline items

What is an outline?

An outline is **a summary of what is contained in a larger project**, like an essay, research paper, a book or a presentation. They are structured by levels, biggest to smallest called a Hierarchy.

Outline Styles

Outlines traditionally start with capital Roman Numerals and a period. The next level is usually capital Arabic letters and a period. In the next level, Arabic numbers are used and next lowercase Arabic letters. If a fifth level is needed (rare), lowercase Roman numerals are used.

Old-fashioned outline style

I. Level 1
    A. Level 2
        1. Level 3
            a) Level 4
                (1) Level 5

Unfortunately, this traditional style is not the default style for outline numbering in Word. The default style is below. It starts with Arabic numbers. This is what we will use for our outline, because to make a heading outline style is beyond the level of this book.

Default outline style in Word

1) Level 1
    a) Level 2
        i) Level 3
            (1) Level 4
                (a) Level 5

Step-By-Step

Follow the steps below to create an outline.

1) Open Microsoft Word 2019:
   a) In Windows 10, click the **Start** button OR in the Search box type **Word 2019**
   b) Click on **Word 2019**
2) Start a blank document:

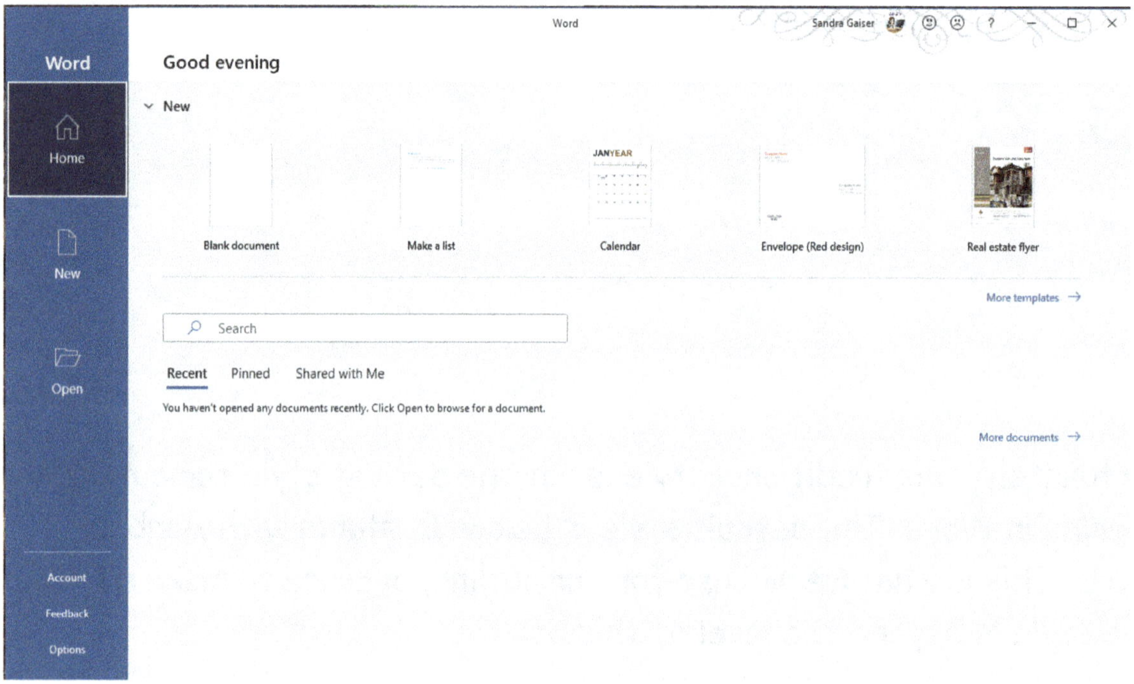

   a) Click on **Blank Document**
3) Title the outline:
   a) Click the **Center** button in the **Paragraph** group on the **Ribbon**.
   b) Type in the name of your animal and "Outline" (example: Blue Whale Outline)
   c) Press **Enter**

d) Click the **Align Text Left** button on the **Ribbon**

4) <u>Choose the outline style:</u>

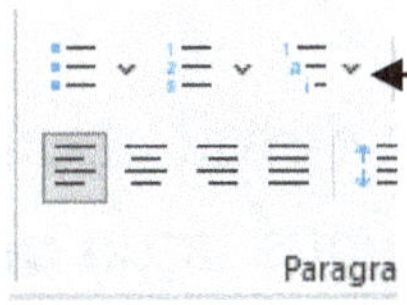

Multilevel list button

a) Click on the **Home** tab, in the **Paragraph** group, click on the **Multilevel List** button.

b) Click on the first numbering style next to **None**.

5) <u>Now, to type in 3 main characteristics about your animal:</u>

a) For the Blue Whale example, I would type in

i) Big (press **Enter**)

ii) Blue (press **Enter**)

iii) Mammal (press **Enter** 2 times to end outline)

6) <u>Let's add 3 details for each main characteristic:</u>

a) Click at the end of the 1st characteristic and press **Enter**.

b) Now you must DEMOTE the level of this detail, so press **TAB** once.

c) Type in the 1st detail about the 1st characteristic (Blue Whale example: 89-110 feet long)

d) Press **Enter** (notice that you stay on that level of the outline)

e) Type in the 2nd detail about the 1st characteristic (Blue Whale example: 200 tons, maximum)

f) Press **Enter**

g) Type in the 3rd detail about the 1st characteristic (Blue Whale example: Birth weight 3 tons)

h) DON'T PRESS ENTER

i) Click at the end of the 2nd characteristic and press **Enter**.

j) Now you must DEMOTE the level of this detail, so press **TAB** once.

k) Type in the 1st detail about the 2nd characteristic (Blue Whale example: Light or dark gray on surface)

l) Press **Enter** (notice that you stay on that level of the outline)

- m) Type in the 2nd detail about the 2nd characteristic (Blue Whale example: Sometime blue on surface)
- n) Press **Enter**
- o) Type in the 3rd detail about the 2nd characteristic (Blue Whale example: Luminous aqua blue under water)
- p) DON'T PRESS ENTER
- q) Click at the end of the 3rd characteristic and press **Enter**.
- r) Now you must DEMOTE the level of this detail, so press **TAB** once.
- s) Type in the 1st detail about the 3rd characteristic (Blue Whale example: Has live babies)
- t) Press **Enter** (notice that you stay on that level of the outline)
- u) Type in the 2nd detail about the 3rd characteristic (Blue Whale example: Nurses babies)
- v) Press **Enter**
- w) Type in the 3rd detail about the 3rd characteristic (Blue Whale example: Warm-blooded)
- x) DON'T PRESS ENTER

7) <u>Make the font size bigger:</u>
   - a) Select all the text (press CTRL-A)
   - b) Increase the font size, about 20 (just make sure the lines don't wrap out of alignment)
   - c) Change the font style if you like

8) <u>Now, add a picture of your animal:</u>
   - a) Click **Insert** tab
   - b) Click **Online Pictures**
   - c) Click on a photo to select it
   - d) Click **Insert**
   - e) Change the text wrapping
     - i) Click on the picture
     - ii) Click on the **Format** tab on the **Ribbon**

iii)Click on **Text Wrapping** in the **Arrange** group.
iv) Choose **In front of text**
v) Drag the picture wherever you want it

9) When you have finished, print the form:
   a) Click **File**
   b) Click **Print**
   c) Click **Print**
10) To save the file:
   a) Click **File**
   b) Click **Save As**
   c) Type in Your name and project name (example: Nick's outline).
   d) Click **Save** button

Lesson 17 Practice

Day 1

1. Follow the steps to make another outline for an English paper.

2. Print it out.

Lesson Review:

1. What is an outline?

____

2. What can you use an outline for?

____

3. What kind of numbers do outlines usually start with?

   ____

4. What kind of numbers does the DEFAULT outline style in Word start with?

   ____

Planning for our next lesson:

1. **Think of a place you of which you like to create a map. It can be a real place or a land from a storybook:** (a country, a state, or magical a land). It must have rivers, flat lands, cities & mountains.

   Name of place:

   ____

2. **Bring a topographical or "topo" map of the place you are going to paint on a map or make sure you know the internet link to a place with a map. That way it will be much easier to paint.**

Lesson 18

18-Paint a Map in Paint

Use paint to paint a map for a history or geography project!

About Our Project

This project will show you how to paint a map. Remember, Microsoft Paint works like a real painter, and has fewer chances to undo. SO, pick a country, state, province or hemisphere and let's get painting!

What you will learn

- Review of Microsoft Paint
- Review of painting tools in Paint

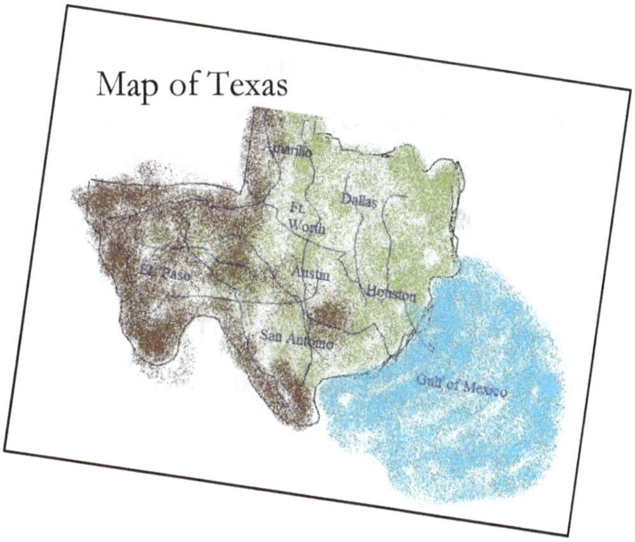

A map painting

We are going to make a painting of a map of a place that we are familiar with or need to for history or geography class. A map should have a recognizable shape outline: Draw this in black. Then, paint in **green where grasslands** would be, **brown for desserts**, little upside-down v's for mountains, **blue areas for oceans, lakes and rivers**.

Follow these steps to paint a map:

1. Use a black line to draw the outline of the shape of your map
2. Then paint in the largest colored areas (usually blue water or green grass areas)
3. Then paint in the smaller colored area (blue rivers, mountains, etc.)
4. Finally, use text boxes to label the cities
5. Use a BIG text box to put the name of the map across the top

Let's get painting!

Step-By-Step

Follow the steps below to paint a map using Microsoft Paint in Windows 10.

1) Open Microsoft Paint:
   a) In Windows 10, click the **Start** button OR in the Search box type **Paint**
   b) Click **Paint (not Paint 3D)**
2) Maximize your work area:
   a) Click in the upper-right hand corner on the middle square to the left of the red X to maximize the program window.

b) Hover your mouse over the lower-right hand corner of the white painting canvas, and drag it down to the lower right edge of the window. This gives you the most area to paint in.

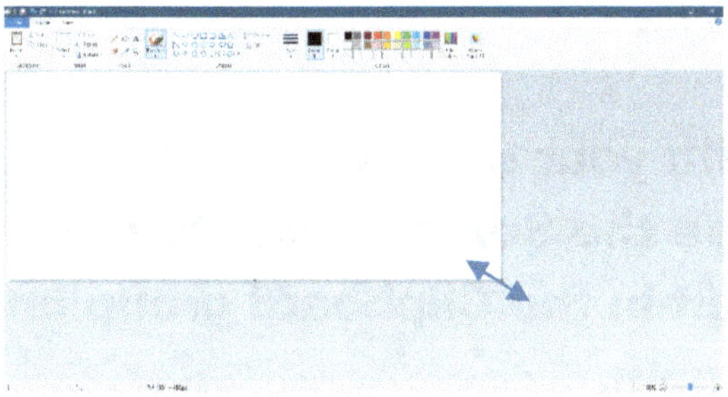
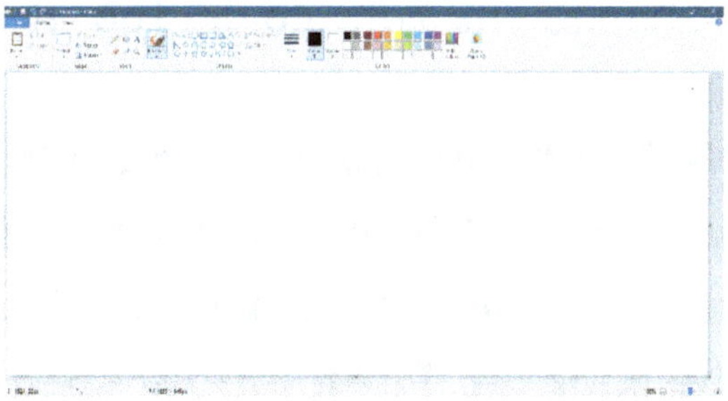

3) Begin your drawing:
   a) Start with the black pencil tool (it should be set for you already), and draw an outline of your map.
4) Sketch in the geographic areas:
   a) Draw the mountains, deserts, oceans, lakes, rivers
   b) Click **Brushes**, **Airbrush**
   c) Click the color you want to spray on
   d) Hold your mouse button down and wiggle your mouse over the areas on your painting to color them

If you make a mistake, click the Undo button as soon as possible.

5) Label important places:
   a) Draw little text boxes and type in name of places and geographic items (Example: Lake Erie, Rocky Mountains, Istanbul, Paris, etc.)
   b) Click the **Text** tool (A)
   c) Click on the **Black** color
   d) Type your label in the box
   e) The box will be transparent (see-through) by default, so you can see your map through the box. If you want the box to have a solid white background, click the **Opaque** button

f) Select all your text and click **B** to make the text Bold
g) Increase or decrease the font size so that the text fits on your painting
h) Change the font color, too, if you like

<u>NOTE:</u> If you make a mistake with your text box, you will have to cut it and re-create it. Use the Select arrow to draw a box around the text box. Click Cut in the Clipboard group on the Ribbon. Then follow step 5 again.

6) <u>When you have finished, print the painting:</u>
   a) Click the **blue File button**
   b) Click **Print**
   c) Click **Print**

Blue File Button

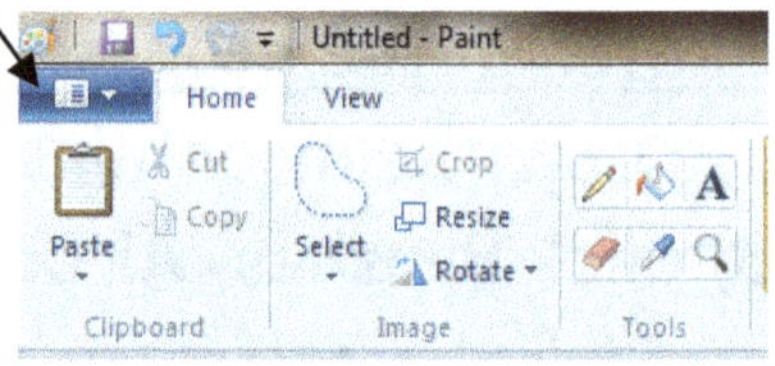

7) <u>To save the file:</u>
   a) Click the **blue File button**
   b) Click **Save As**
   c) Type in Your name and project name (example: Nick's map)
   d) Click **Save** button.

Lesson 18 Practice

Day 1

1. Follow the steps to paint another map for a history or geography lesson.

2. Print it out.

Lesson Review:

1. What tool should you use to draw the map outline shape?

   ____

2. What is a good tool to use to paint rivers?

   ____

3. What button makes a solid white background in the text boxes?

   ____

Planning for our next lesson:

1. **We will be writing a poem, so you may want to bring your favorite children's thesaurus to class with you.**

2. **What words best describe you?**

   __________ __________ __________

   __________ __________ __________

   __________ __________ __________

Lesson
19

19-An Acrostic Name Poem in Word

A really fun poem to make all about you!

About Our Project

We are going to use Microsoft Word to make an acrostic poem using your name. It will be all about you, describing you with adjectives that begin with letters in your name. Try to **pick at least 3 words** for each line. And **you can even make up words** like "apple-loving"! So, have fun with it!

S sassy, summery, sunny, simple
A artsy, antsy, apple-loving
N nice, neat, nimble
D dancing, delightful
R racy, red
A all-done!

What you will learn

- How to change font sizes
- How to change font styles
- How to use the Format Painter
- How to use the Repeat Key (F4)

The Acrostic Poem

> An acrostic (from the late Greek akróstichis, from ákros, "top", and stíchos, "verse") is a poem or other form of writing in an alphabetic script, in which the first letter, syllable or word of each line, paragraph or other recurring feature in the text spells out a word or a message.

Source: Wikipedia, website: en.wikipedia.org/wiki/Acrostic

In this project, **the letters at the beginning of each line will spell your name**! Now, you will have to be creative and think of lots of adjectives and adverbs (describing words) to put after each letter of your name. And you can **make up words**! These words should describe **you**:

Adverbs Adjectives

- Your personality
- Your favorite things
- Funny things about you
- Games or sports you play

smart

beautiful

serious

loving

kind

intelligent

strong

faithful

funny

Art-loving

hard-working

Step-By-Step

Follow the steps below to create an Acrostic Name Poem with your name.

1) <u>Open Microsoft Word 2019:</u>
   a) In Windows 10, click the **Start** button OR in the Search box type **Word 2019**
   b) Click **Word 2019**
2) <u>Type in all the letters of your name vertically:</u>
   a) Set the font size to 32 in the **Font** Group on the **Ribbon**
      i) Click inside the **Font Size** box right on top of the numbers
      ii) Type **32**
   b) Type the 1st letter of your name
   c) Press **Tab** on your keyboard
   d) Press **Enter** key
   e) Type the 2nd letter of your name
   f) Press Tab on your keyboard
   g) Press **Enter** key
   h) Type the 3rd letter of your name
   i) Press **Tab** on your keyboard
   j) Press **Enter** key.
   k) Continue like this until you have typed all the letters in your first name.

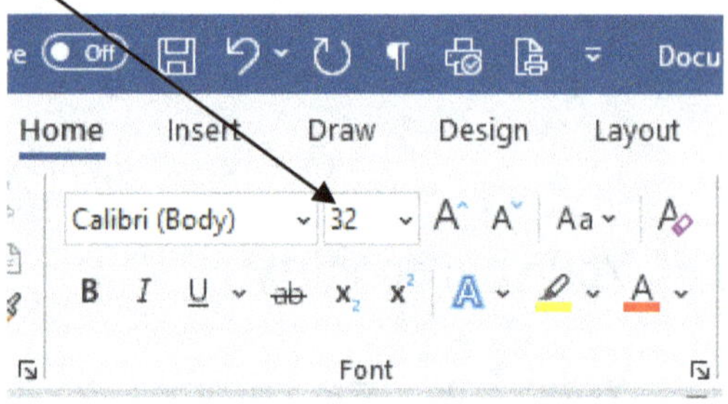

Note: If your first name is very short, press Enter again after your first name and continue with all the letters of your middle or last name.

3) <u>Now we will add the adjectives that describe you next to each letter:</u>

a) Turn on your **Show/Hide** button, if it's not on, to see the **Tabs** you made. Click the  in the **Paragraph** group on the **Home** tab on the **Ribbon**.

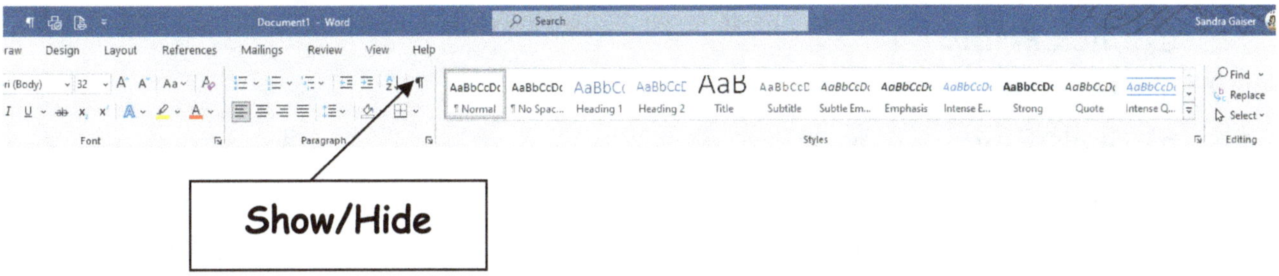

b) Click your mouse to the right of the 1st letter of your name after the **Tab** (➔)
c) Change the font size to 14
d) Type in an adjective that begins with that letter
e) Then type a **comma**
f) Press the **Spacebar**
g) Do steps (d), and (e) two more times. You should have 3 words after your letter now.
h) Now, do steps **3b-g** for the remaining letters of your name.

4) <u>To change to font of your poem:</u>
   a) Press **CTRL-A** to select all the text
   b) Choose the font style you want on the **Ribbon** on the **Home** tab in the **Font** group. As you hover over each font you will be able to preview what it looks like on your page.

5) <u>To change the font color of your poem:</u>
   a) Press **CTRL-A** to select all the text
   b) Choose the font color you want on the **Ribbon** on the **Home** tab in the **Font** group. Click the tiny black arrow to the right of the Font Color button 

c) Choose your font color

6) When you have finished, print your poem:

a) Click **File**

b) Click **Print**

c) Click **Print**

7) To save the poem:

a) Click **File**

b) Click **Save As**

c) Type in Your name and project name (example: Nick's poem)

d) Click **Save** button

Lesson 19 Practice

Day 1

1. Follow the steps and make an Acrostic Name Poem for someone in your family.

2. Print it out.

3. Give it to them!

Lesson Review:

1. What is a thesaurus?

   ____

2. What is a synonym?

   ____

3. What does the Show/Hide button do?

   ____

Planning for our next lesson:

1. **We will be working with computer images of all types. You can bring some of your favorite photos or images on your computer or flash drive to class to use.**
2. **If you have a digital camera or camera phone, you can bring it to class, but make sure you BRING THE CABLE so we can connect it to the computer and download the pictures to work with.**

Lesson

20

20-Editing Photos with Word

A wonderful program to edit, resize and enhance your photos!

About Our Project

We are going to learn about working with digital pictures using Microsoft Office. You can edit pictures from within any Microsoft Office program.: Word, Excel, PowerPoint, Publisher, OneNote, Sway or Outlook. We are going to use Word.

What you will learn

- What a digital photo is
- What Picture Manager is
- How to use photo editing tools
- How to crop a photo

A digital photo

We are going work with digital photos, but first you need to learn what they are made of so that you can work with them. Every digital photo is made up of tiny pixels.

Photo pixel: *It is the smallest unit of picture that can be represented or controlled*

Pixel is short for **picture element**. It means the smallest part of a photo that you can mess around with.

Low resolution: In the 1980's, digital cameras had very few pixels in a photo: 1.4 million to be exact. Today, this is called "low resolution". That means when you stretch or enlarge the photo, it becomes fuzzy or "**pixelated**". You can clearly **see** the tiny squares of the photo.

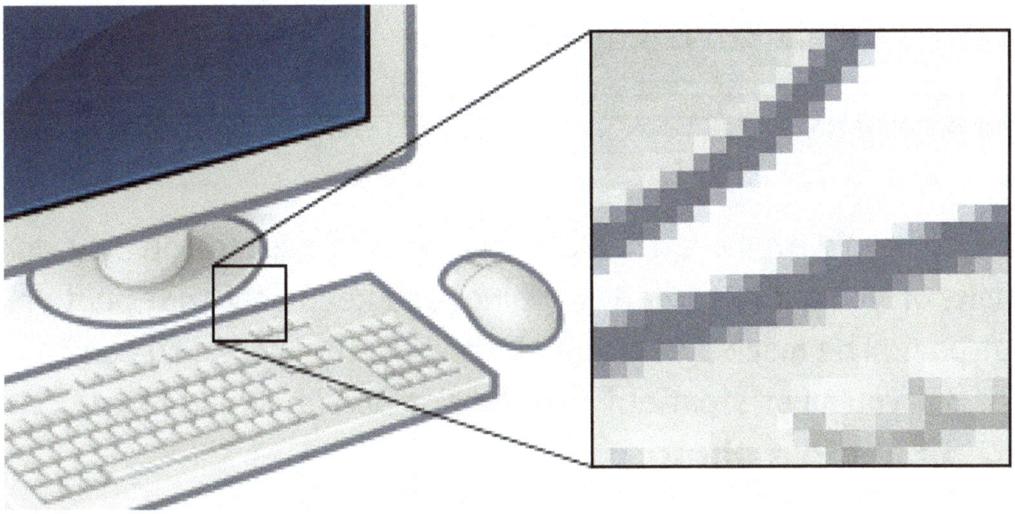

Source: Wikipedia: http://en.wikipedia.org/wiki/Pixel

High resolution: Digital cameras these days take photos with multi-millions of pixels in them. The more pixels there are, the more you can enlarge or stretch the photo. See below:

Camera size	Pixels per photo	Maximum size high quality photo
1.4 megapixel	1,400,000 million	3 x 5 or online photos
2 megapixels	2 million (1600 x 1200)	4 x 6 or 5 x 7
3 megapixels	3 million (2048 x 1546)	8 x 10
5 megapixels	5 million (2592 x 1944)	10 x 13
Anything bigger		Up to poster size

So why get a camera with more than 5 megapixels? Because you may want to cut out chunks of you photo (called cropping) and keep only that part or enlarge that part. The more pixels you start with, the more you can cut out and stretch. But you must start out with lots of pixels because **you can never ADD pixels to a photo**.

Cropping: To cut out parts of the photo that you don't want, or to zoom in on parts that you do want.

Cropping

Sometimes you may want only part of a photo or cut out some parts of a photo that don't belong. We'll do this, too.

Step-By-Step

Follow the steps below to edit a photo using Microsoft Word. We will make 6 copies of the same photo with 6 different edits.

1) <u>Open Microsoft Word 2019:</u>
   a) In Windows 10, click the **Start** button OR in the Search box type **Word 2019**
   b) Click **Word 2019**
2) <u>Click on Blank document</u>
3) <u>Insert a picture to edit:</u>
   a) Click **Insert**, **Pictures**

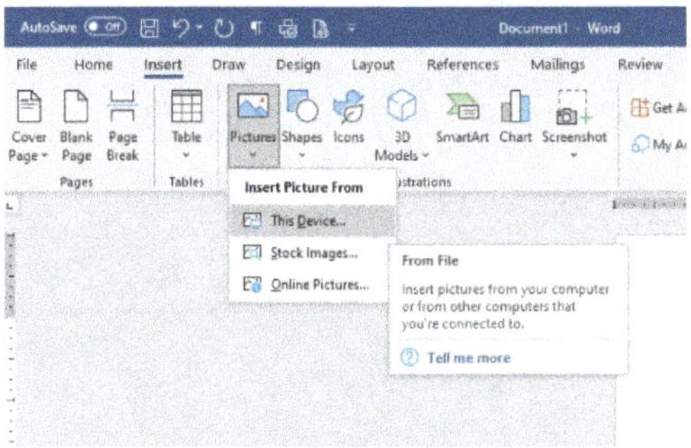

This will take you into the Pictures folder on your computer. You should have some pictures stored here. If not, browse to a folder or your flash drive where you do have some pictures.

   b) **Double-click** on any photo to insert it onto the page.
4) <u>First, let's see the photo's pixels:</u>
   a) Pull the **Zoom** slider at the bottom-right corner of the screen to the right until you can see the little squares or pixels that make up the photo. Cool, huh?
   b) Now drag the slider back towards the minus until the photo is a good size to see all of it.
5) <u>To edit the photo:</u>
   a) Make sure the photo is selected by clicking on it

b) On the Ribbon, click on the **Picture Tools Format** contextual tab

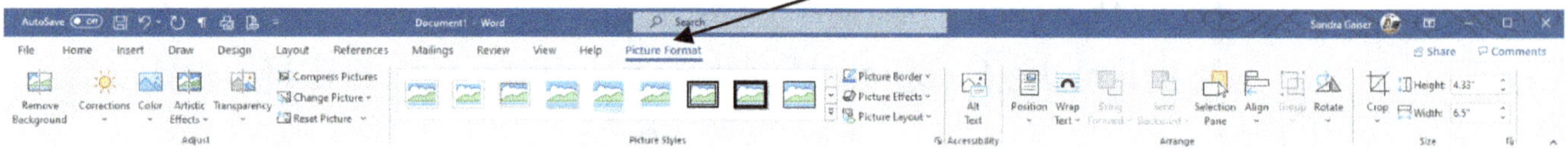

6) First let's try the **Remove Background** button:

a) With the photo selected, click the first button on the Ribbon, **Remove Background**.

b) Click **Keep Changes**

Word will automatically select most of the background in the photo to be removed (this can be changed by using the Mark Areas to Keep / Mark Areas to Remove buttons).

c) Let's save this first photo:

i) Right-click on the photo

ii) Click **Save as Picture**

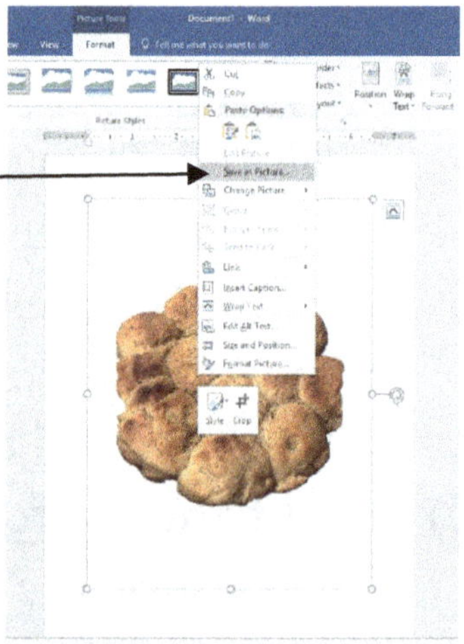

iii) Choose the folder to save it into

iv) Name it ***Your Name No Background Pic***

v) Click **Save**

7) OK, let's Reset the photo back to its original form:

a) Click **Reset Picture** in the **Adjust** group on the **Ribbon**.

8) Now, to change the brightness & contrast in the picture:
   a) Click the **Corrections** button on the **Ribbon**.
   b) Hover over each of the preset options to see them applied to your photo.
   c) Let's see more options, slide all the way down to **Picture Correction Options** and click.
   d) Slide the **Sharpness**, **Brightness** & **Contrast** sliders to make your photo look REALLY different!
   e) Let's save this 2nd photo:
      i) Right-click on the photo
      ii) Click **Save as Picture**
      iii) Choose the folder to save it into
      iv) Name it ***Your Name Corrections Pic***
      v) Click **Save**

You can UNDO anything you try with a photo. Click Undo.

9) OK, let's Reset the photo back to its original form again:
   a) Click **Reset Picture** in the **Adjust** group on the **Ribbon**.

10) Now click on **Color** and try the color settings:
   a) Hover all the different colors
   b) Try the **Grayscale** option (this is how you make a photo black and white)
   c) Make your photo look REALLY different!
   d) Let's save this 3rd photo:
      i) Right-click on the photo
      ii) Click **Save as Picture**
      iii) Choose the folder to save it into
      iv) Name it ***Your Name Color Pic***
      v) Click **Save**

11) <u>OK, let's Reset the photo back to its original form again:</u>
    a) Click **Reset Picture** in the **Adjust** group on the **Ribbon**.
12) <u>Now try the Artistic Effects:</u>
    a) Click **Artistic Effects**
    b) Hover over all the different styles
    c) Make your photo look REALLY different!
    d) <u>Let's save this 4th photo:</u>
        i) Right-click on the photo
        ii) Click **Save as Picture**
        iii) Choose the folder to save it into
        iv) Name it ***Your Name Art Pic***
        v) Click **Save**

13) <u>OK, let's Reset the photo back to its original form again:</u>
    a) Click **Reset Picture** in the **Adjust** group on the **Ribbon**.
14) <u>Now click on **Crop** and try cropping your photo:</u>
    a) Hover over the black dashes on the sides and corners of the photos and click and drag them in to cut off part of the photo. Make your photo look REALLY different!
    b) Click off the photo when you are done.
    c) <u>Let's save this 5th photo:</u>
        i) Right-click on the photo
        ii) Click **Save as Picture**
        iii) Choose the folder to save it into
        iv) Name it ***Your Name Crop Pic***
        v) Click **Save**

15) <u>OK, let's Reset the photo back to its original form again:</u>
    a) Click **Reset Picture** in the **Adjust** group on the **Ribbon**.
16) <u>Now click on **Rotate** and rotate and flip your photo:</u>
    a) **Flip Horizontal** is great for getting a mirror image. Try it!

b) **Flip Vertical** can fix or make an upside-down photo.

c) Let's save this 6th photo:

  i) Right-click on the photo

  ii) Click ***Save as Picture***

  iii) Choose the folder to save it into

  iv) Name it ***Your Name Flip Pic***

  v) Click ***Save***

You can also Compress Pictures with the compression settings. This is very helpful to reduce the density (and file size) of a photo when you don't need photo quality. It reduces the pixels, so never do this to an original photo without backing it up first.

17) When you have finished, print the photos with the Windows Photo Printing Wizard:

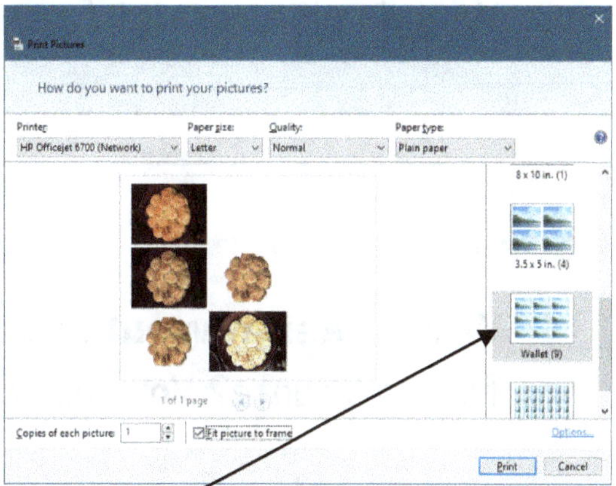

a) Close **Word** and don't save the document.

b) Open the folder where you saved all 6 photos you made.

c) Hold the **CTRL** key down and click on all 6 photos.

d) Let go of the **CTRL** key

e) Right-click on the selected photos

f) Click **Print**

g) Change the settings as you want

h) Scroll down on the right and click **Wallet** to fit all the photos on one sheet of paper

i) Click **Print**

Lesson 20 Practice

Day 1

1. **Follow the steps to edit some other photos. Have fun!**
2. **Print them out.**

Lesson Review:

1. What is pixel?

   ____

2. How many pixels in a 5-megapixel picture?

   ____

3. Why do pictures get fuzzy-looking when you zoom in?

   ____

Planning for our next lesson:

1. **What design would you like to put on a t-shirt?** Words? A favorite quote? Your name? A picture?

   ____

2. **Write down some things you would see in your favorite season.** Snowman? Rain? Fall leaves? A water skier?

   ________ ________ ________

Lesson

21

21-Making T-Shirt transfers in Publisher

Make your own t-shirts that say or show anything you want!

About Our Project

We are going to make a design in Publisher to print on a t-shirt. Make sure you print on a light-colored t-shirt. You can print t-shirt transfers on dark t-shirts, but you will need special paper for that, and the process is more complicated, so we will stick with light fabric transfers today. So, think of great design, and let's go!

What you will learn

- What a t-shirt transfer is
- How to make a design in Publisher
- What Copyright is

What is a t-shirt transfer?

A t-shirt transfer is made by **printing a cool, computer-made design on special t-shirt transfer paper**, and then ironing that transfer onto a t-shirt. Voila! You made your own custom t-shirt.

Can be ironed on more than t-shirts

You can also iron the transfer onto a cotton bag or a hat. You can find these items at hobby stores.

There are 2 kinds of t-shirt transfer paper:

- For light fabrics
- For dark fabrics

Make sure you match the right transfers you use to the right fabric you put them on. There are **VERY DIFFERENT PRINTING STEPS** for each type of transfer paper.

Use the page space wisely

Transfer paper is relatively large and expensive, so make sure you the space on your page wisely. You can make 1 very large image or 2 medium-size images on the top and bottom of your page, or 3 or 4 smaller images for pocket-size transfers. You can cut the transfer paper any way you choose:

Copyrighted images

You can put any image or picture you want on your t-shirt but **beware of copyright laws**!

> **Copyright is a creator's right to not have his or her creations copied and used by other people without permission from the creator.**

You <u>may not</u> put a copyrighted design on an item like a t-shirt, bag or hat and sell it. Any original artwork created in the United States is automatically copyrighted to the creator or that artwork. SO, every time YOU create something that no one else has exactly created before, you own the copyright to it!

SO, be CREATIVE with your transfer design! Make something new and exciting! Be bold!

If you would like more information on copyright law, go to https://www.youtube.com/watch?v=Sjf6l2X4qJU.

Use WordArt for words

WORDART IS FUN!

There are 2 reasons to use WordArt for the words you put on your transfer:

1. WordArt **makes text look fantastic**!
2. WordArt actually **converts text into an image** and that makes it easy to rotate horizontally, which you have to do before you print out your light transfer

Here are some inspirational short quotes:

Dare to Win	Be Yourself	Never give up
Believe in yourself	Follow your dreams	Seize the day
Life is awesome	Be inspired	Be the change
Success is yours	I can do it	My mind rules
Believe you can	Thought is free - William Shakespeare	

Step-By-Step

Follow the steps below to create a light t-shirt transfer in Microsoft Publisher.

1) Open Microsoft Publisher 2019:
   a) In Windows 10, click the **Start** button OR in the Search box type **Publisher 2019**
   b) Click **Publisher 2019**
2) Choose blank paper:
   a) Double-click on **Blank 8.5 x 11"** (portrait) or **11 x 8.5"** (landscape)
3) Let's add stuff like we've learned:
   a) Insert **WordArt**
   b) Insert **Online Photos**
   c) Insert images

Don't insert text boxes because it can't be flipped. Use only WordArt for words.

4) When you have finished, print the page:

a) 1st, print the design on a plain piece of paper first to see how it looks, and to see what side of the paper it prints on.
b) Insert the t-shirt transfer paper PROPERLY into your printer. (See your printer documentation if necessary or you will print on the wrong side of the paper.)
c) Click **File**
d) Make sure your print settings are for t-shirt transfer paper type (this varies per printer) or photo paper.
e) Click **Print**
f) Click **Print**

5) <u>To save the file:</u>
a) Click **File**
b) Click **Save As**
c) Type in Your name and project name (example: Nick's t-shirt).
d) Click **Save** button

6) To iron on the transfer, follow the EXACT directions from the t-shirt transfer paper box.

Lesson 21 Practice

Day 1

1. Follow the steps to make another t-shirt transfer for someone else.

2. Print it out.

3. Give it away!

Lesson Review:

1. What is WordArt?

    ____

2. What is a copyright?

    ____

3. Are your creations copyrighted?

    ____

Planning for our next lesson:

We are going to type up a book report based on a book you have already read. Fill in the following information so you will be ready to type up your report in the next class:

1. Book title:

    ____

2. Book Author (who wrote it):

    ____

3. Book Illustrator (who drew the pictures):

    ____

4. Story setting (where & when it took place):

    Location:

    ____

Years/season/dates /era

____

Country/city/state

____

5. Characters (people in the book):

____________ ____________ ____________

____________ ____________ ____________

6. Conflict (problem in the story): ____________________

____

7. Conclusion (how it all turned out): ____________________

____

____

8. Would you recommend the book to someone? Yes No

Why? ____________________________________

____

____

Lesson
22

22-Writing a book report in Word

A fun format to show what you've read!

About Our Project

We are going to make a book report in Word. More and more, people are relying on computers for written material, especially school papers.

What you will learn

- What a book report is
- How to gather information for a book report
- How to center a title
- How to add a border
- How to make newspaper columns in Word

The Very Hungry Caterpillar

by Nicholas Mortensen

This book was written by Eric Carle.

The pictures were also drawn by Eric Carle

The only character in this book is a very hungry caterpillar.

The problem this caterpillar faces was his incredible hunger because he was growing so fast.

Throughout the book, the caterpillar ate everything he came across and was finally filled up enough to make his cocoon and turn into a beautiful butterfly.

I really enjoyed this book because it was brightly colored, short and really cute. It made me happy and made me laugh

A book report

A book report is something you write to show what you have learned from reading a book. **You need to know the following items before you write your book report**. Make sure you have this form completed first:

Book title: ______________________________

Book Author (who wrote it): ______________________________

Book Illustrator (who drew the pictures): ______________________________

Story setting (where it took place):

Location: ______________________________

Years/season/dates /era: ______________________________

Country/city/state: ______________________________

Characters (people in the book):

______________ ______________ ______________

Conflict (problem in the story): ______________________________

____

Conclusion (how it all turned out): ______________________________

____

Would you recommend the book to someone? Yes No

Why? ______________________________

Your book report will have 6 paragraphs when it is finished. Your paragraphs can be as long or as short as you like. You will put them in this order:

The title:
The name of the book you read

The Byline:
Your name

The Author & Illustrator:

The Setting:
Where it happens

Characters:
Who's in the book

The Problem:
What's wrong?

The Solution:
How is it fixed?

Your Review:
Did you like it or not?

The Very Hungry Caterpillar

By: Mrs. Gaiser

The book was written by Eric Carle. He also drew the pictures.

The setting of the book was in a tree probably in the spring.

The only character in the book is a very hungry caterpillar,

The problem this caterpillar faces was his incredible hunger because he was growing so fast.

Throughout the book, the caterpillar ate everything he came across and was finally filled up enough to make his cocoon and turn in a beautiful butterfly.

I really enjoyed this book because it was brightly colored, short and really cute. It made me happy and made me laugh.

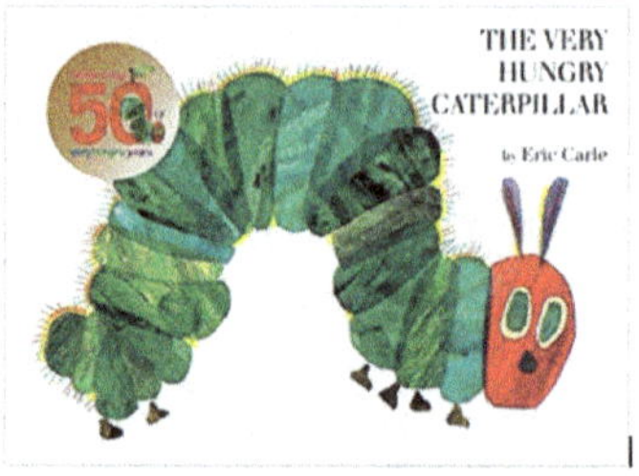

Step-By-Step

Follow the steps below to create a newspaper style book report in Microsoft Word.

1) Open Microsoft Word:
   a) In Windows 10, click the **Start** button  OR in the Search box type **Word 2019**
   b) Click **Word 2019**
2) Click on Blank document
3) Title the book report:
   a) Click the **Center** button in the **Paragraph** group on the **Ribbon**
   b) Type in the title of your book (If you don't know the title yet, just type the word **TITLE** for now, then type it in later.)
   c) Press **Enter**
   d) Click on the **Align Left** button in the **Paragraph** group on the **Ribbon**
   e) Press **Enter**

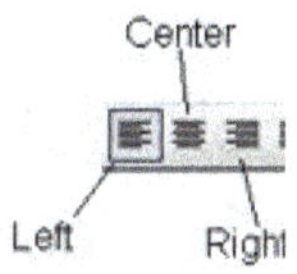

Text Alignment buttons

4) Now let's set up newspaper columns:
   a) 1st you need to break the page into sections:
      i) Click on the **Layout** tab
      ii) Click on **Breaks**
      iii) Click on **Continuous**
   b) Turn on your Show/Hide to see the break you just added
      i) Click on the **Home** tab
      ii) Click on the **Show/Hide** button  in the **Paragraph** group
   c) Turn on the columns:
      i) Click the **Layout** tab on the **Ribbon**

ii) Click on **Columns** in the Page Setup group
iii) Click on **More Columns**
iv) Click on **Two**
v) Check the **Line Between** box
vi) Click **OK**

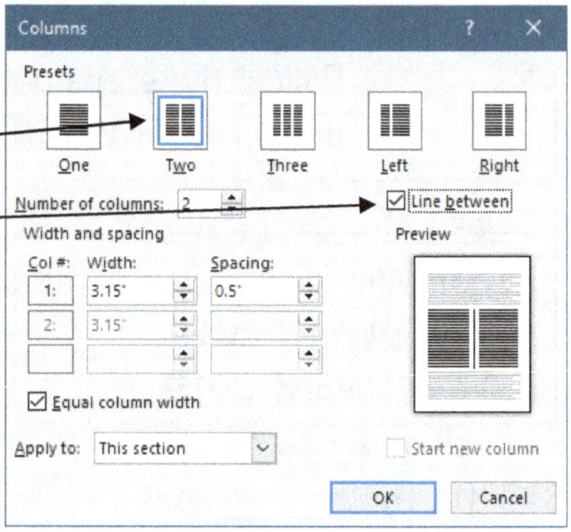

5) <u>Now let's finish typing your book report:</u>
   a) Set the font size bigger:
      i) Press **CTRL-A** to select all the text on the page
      ii) Set the font size to 14
   b) Type in **By: (Your Name)** because you are the author of this report
   c) Press **Enter**
6) Type your 1st paragraph about who wrote the book: the author. (Example: *This book was written by Eric Carle.*)
   a) Press **Enter**.
7) Type your 2nd paragraph about where the book took place: the setting. (Example: *The pictures were also drawn by Eric Carle.*)
   a) Press **Enter**
8) Type your 3rd paragraph about the important people in the book: the characters. (Example: *The only character in this book is a very hungry caterpillar.*)
   a) Press **Enter**
9) Type your 4th paragraph about problem the characters faced: the plot. (Example: *The problem this caterpillar faced was his incredible hunger because he was growing so fast.*)
   a) Press **Enter**
10) Type your 5th paragraph about how the problem was solved and how the book ended: the solution. (Example: *Throughout the book, the*

caterpillar ate everything he came across and was finally filled up enough to make his cocoon and turn into a beautiful butterfly.)

a) Press **Enter**

11) Type your 6th paragraph about whether or not you liked the book and why: the review. (Example: *I really enjoyed this book because it was brightly colored, short and really cute.)*

a) Press **Enter**

12) <u>Now to make the title look nicer:</u>

a) Click anywhere in the title.

b) Click the **Bottom Border** button on the **Home** tab on the **Ribbon** in the **Paragraph** group.

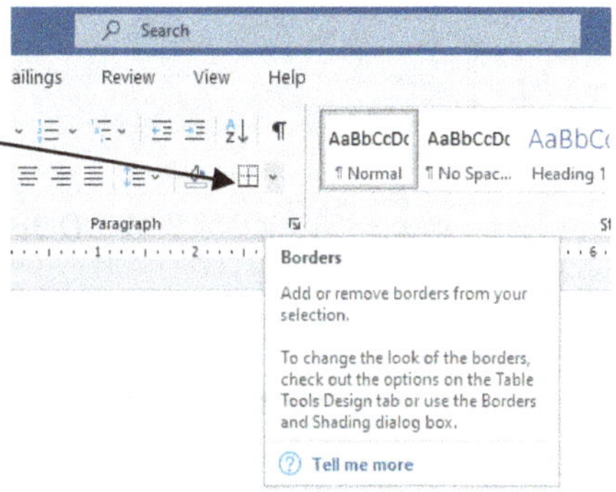

c) Select all the words in the title.

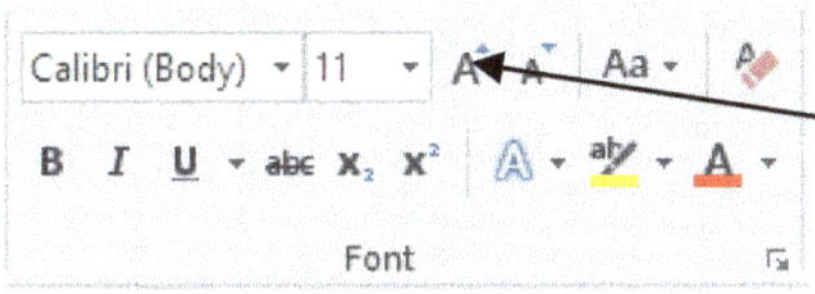

d) Using the **Increase Font Size** button on the **Home** tab in the **Font** group, increase the font size until the title fits across the whole page.

13) <u>Insert a picture of the front cover of the book:</u>

a) Click the **Insert** tab, then click **Online Pictures**

b) Search for your book title, click **Insert**

14) <u>When you have finished, print the book report:</u>

a) Click **File**

b) Click **Print**

c) Click **Print**

15) <u>To save the file:</u>

a) Click **File**

b) Click **Save As**

c) Type in Your name and project name (example: Nick's book report).

d) Click **Save** button

Lesson 22 Practice

Day 1

1. Follow the steps to make another book report about another book you have read.

2. Print it out.

Lesson Review:

1. What is a book report used for?

   ____

2. What does an author do?

   ____

3. What does an illustrator do?

   ____

Planning for our next lesson:

1. **Do you know what a chart is?**

   ____

2. **Have you ever made a chart in Excel? Yes No**

Lesson

23

23-Skittles® Chart in Excel

A fun and delicious way to learn how to make graphs in a spreadsheet!

About Our Project

We are going to use Microsoft Excel to make a spreadsheet and then a colorful pie chart of the colors of candies in the bag you have.

What you will learn

- Review what Excel is
- What a chart is

Making a Chart in Excel

Remember, Microsoft Excel is a program that **makes adding up numbers easy and fast**! It also puts information in **neat rows and columns** must easier than Microsoft Word can.

> **The rule is this: if you want to work with numbers, use Excel; if you want to work with words, use Word!**

Excel names its little boxes "**cells**".

The exact **name of a cell** is its location: column name first, then row number. For example: A2 means the little box in column A, row number 2. So, start in column A and go down 2 rows - and there you are on cell A2! Just like in the game Battleship®.

Excel uses those neat rows and columns of numbers to do something else: make charts! Charts of all kinds:

By entering the numbers for your chart in Excel and labeling the columns, Excel can convert those numbers (or data, as it is called) into a chart! Let's make a pie chart of the number of candies you have:

First, we'll enter the "data" like this:

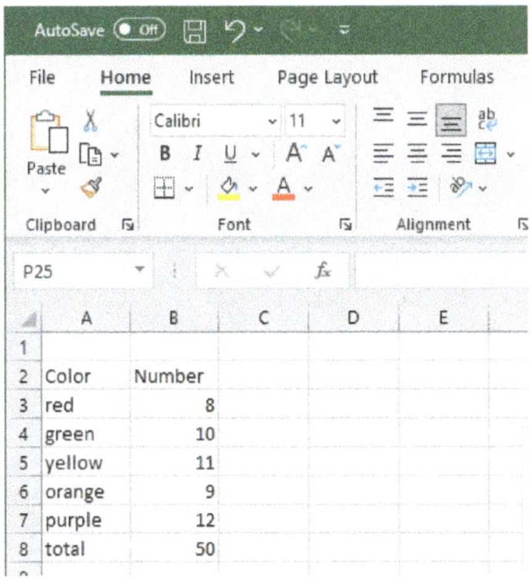

Then we will convert it into a pie chart like this:

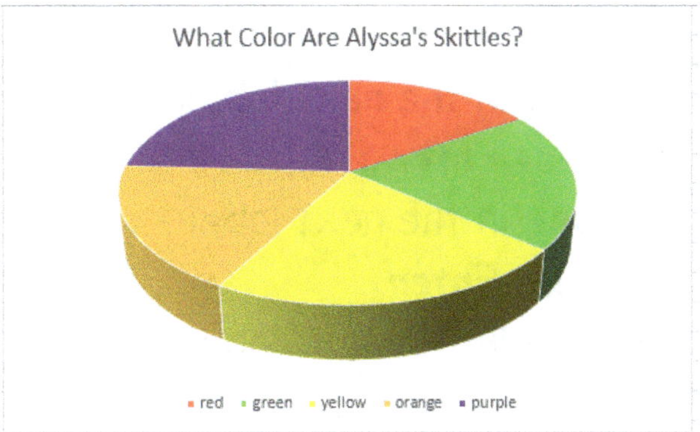

The Pie Chart

A pie chart shows percentages (or parts of 100). So, the best way to show what colors are in our bag of candies is to use a pie chart.

Step-By-Step

Follow the steps below to create a Skittles® Chart in Excel.

1) <u>Open Microsoft Excel 2019:</u>
    a) In Windows 10, click the **Start** button OR in the Search box type **Excel 2019**
    b) Click **Excel 2019**
2) <u>Click on **Blank workbook**</u>
3) <u>Start in cell A3:</u>
    a) Go to column A, go down 3 rows and click in the box (called a cell). This leaves room for the sheet title later.

4) Enter you row titles for the colors of the candies:
   a) Type in your first label: RED
   b) Press **Enter** (the cursor will go down to the next box)
   c) Type in the next label: GREEN
   d) Press **Enter**
   e) Type in the next label: YELLOW
   f) Press **Enter**
   g) Type in the next label: ORANGE
   h) Press **Enter**
   i) Type in the next label: PURPLE
   j) Press **Enter**
5) Enter your column titles:
   a) Start in cell B1, just click on it.
   b) Type in the 1st column label: **COLOR**
   c) Press **Tab** (the cursor will go to the right to cell B2)
   d) Type in the 2nd column label: **NUMBER**
6) Enter the "data" (the number of candies of each color):
   a) Click in cell B3.
   b) Type in the number of RED Skittles® you have.
   c) Press **Enter** to go down to the next cell.
   d) Type in the number of GREEN Skittles® you have.
   e) Press **Enter** to go down to the next cell.
   f) Type in the number of YELLOW Skittles® you have.
   g) Press **Enter** to go down to the next cell.
   h) Type in the number of ORANGE Skittles® you have.
   i) Press **Enter** to go down to the next cell.
   j) Type in the number of PURPLE Skittles® you have.
   k) Press **Enter** to go down to the next cell.

7) <u>Now, make a Pie Chart of your Skittles®</u>
   a) Select (click and drag) over everything you typed in.
   b) Click the **Insert** tab on the **Ribbon**
   c) In the **Charts** groups, click on **Pie**.
   d) Click **3-D Pie** to select it.

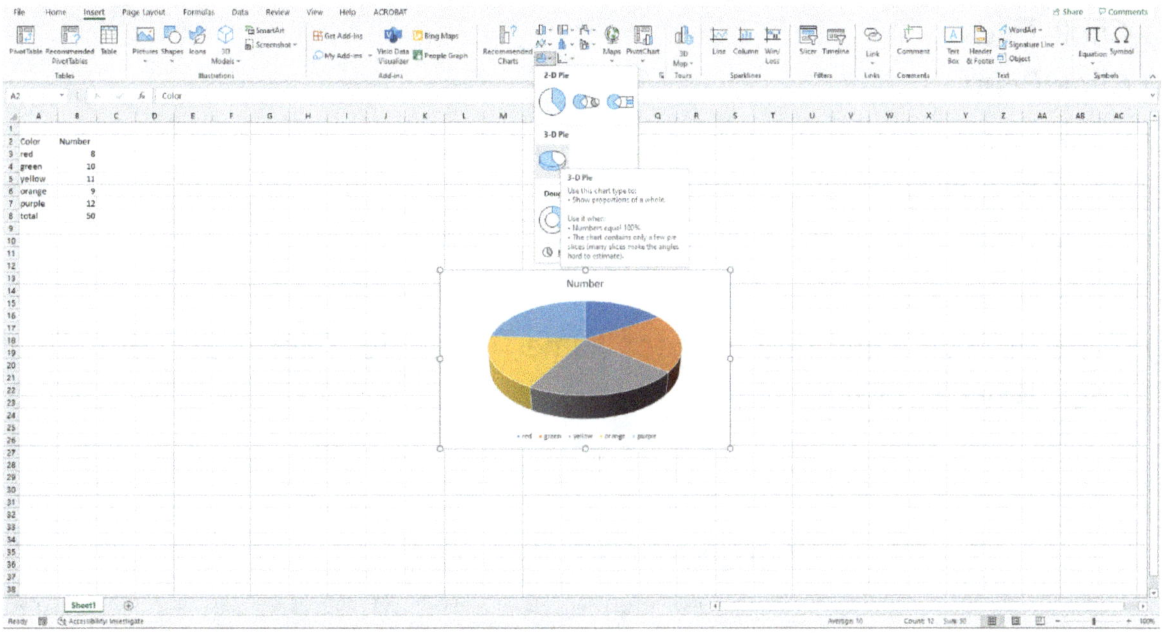

8) <u>Fix the chart to show the right colors to match your Skittles®:</u>
   a) Click the pie section you want to change.
   b) Click it once more (be careful not double-click). This will select only one pie piece.
   c) Now right-click the pie section
   d) Click **Fill** (the little paint can) to choose the color you want. (Match the color to the Skittles®)
   e) Click **OK**.
   f) Repeat steps 8a-g to set the correct color the on other pie slices.
9) <u>Title the chart:</u>

a) Double-click on the chart title at the top of the chart (it should read **Number** right now) to select it.
b) Double-click again to select the text in the box.
c) Type in **Your Name Skittles Chart**
d) Click on the side of the chart anywhere to exit the title box.

10) <u>When you have finished, print the spreadsheet:</u>
a) Click **File**
b) Click **Print**
c) Click **Print**

11) <u>To save the file:</u>
a) Click **File**
b) Click **Save As**
c) Type in Your name and project name (example: Nick's Skittles Chart).
d) Click **Save** button

Lesson 23 Practice

Day 1

1. Try making a chart of some other kind of multi-colored candies.

2. Print it out.

3. Put it in your binder with your other projects this year.

Lesson Review:

1. What is a cell in Excel?

___

2. How does Excel name cells?

___

3. What is a pie chart?

___

Planning for our next lesson:

1. **What events are coming up that you could make a greeting card for?** Birthday, Anniversary, holiday?

___

___

___

Lesson

24

24-Making a Greeting card in Publisher

Make a beautiful greeting card for family and friends!

About Our Project

We are going to use Microsoft Publisher to make a greeting card. Choose someone for which to make the card: grandparents, aunt, uncle, siblings or parents. Now, let's make another greeting card.

What you will learn

- Review how to use a greeting card template
- Review how to change the layout of a greeting card
- Review how to change the color scheme
- Review how to change the font scheme
- Review how to change the verse
- Learn how to change the card size

A Greeting Card

You know Microsoft Publisher has the ability to make all kinds of greeting cards quickly. Remember when we made the Thanksgiving card? Have you made anyone a birthday card since then? I hope so. Many templates are included for holidays and special occasions. You can use the cards the way they are or change any part of them including the words, colors, pictures and styles. Today we are going to learn how to change the card size.

Card Sizes

You can make 2 different card sizes: quarter-fold, like we did before. It fits in an invitation-size envelope. It prints all on 1 side of the paper. Or, half-fold, like the bigger cards at the card shops.

Quarter page side or top fold card:
All sides print on 1 side of the paper

Half page side fold card:
2 sides print on 1 side of the paper and 2 sides print on the other side of the paper.

The trick to half-fold cards is that it's printed on **BOTH sides of the paper**. And you MUST learn how to feed the paper in properly to print the second side. This depends completely on your specific printer. All printers do this differently, so watch carefully how your printer prints so you know how to flip and re-insert the paper. If you have trouble with it (I usually do!), consult your printer's user manual or look online for the steps for your printer.

Step-By-Step

Follow the steps below to create a large Easter card in Microsoft Publisher.

1) Open Microsoft Publisher 2019:
   a) In Windows 10, click the **Start** button OR in the Search box type **Publisher 2019**
   b) Click **Publisher 2019**
2) Open a pre-designed Easter Card template:
   a) Click **BUILT-IN**
   b) Click on **Greeting Cards**
   c) In the **Holidays** row, click on the yellow folder **All Holidays**
   d) Scroll down a few rows to the **Easter** row with 5 Easter templates.
   e) Click **ONCE** on the **Easter** card that you like (don't double-click or you will go right into the publication before you can choose your options)

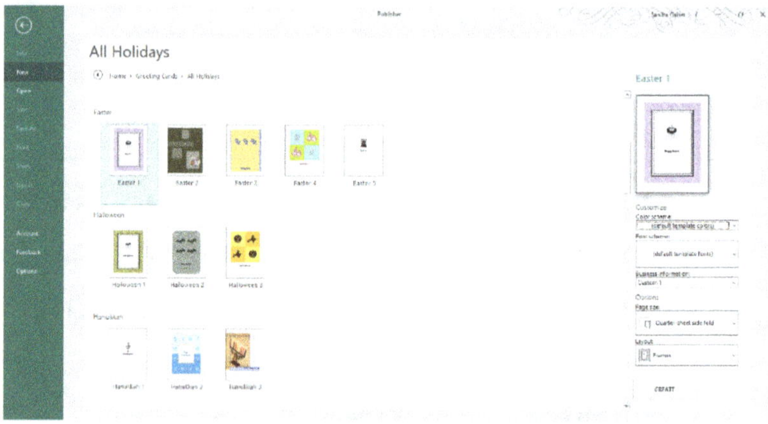

3) In the right pane, customize the card the way you want it:
   a) Change the Color scheme
      i) Click **Color Scheme** on right side
      ii) Click a color scheme you like. Try as many as you like, only the last choice stays.
   b) Change the Font scheme
      i) Click **Font Scheme** on right side
      ii) Click a font scheme you like. Try as many as you like, only the last choice stays.
   c) Change the Page Size of the Card:
      i) Choose **Half-sheet side fold** (prints on both sides of page). Objects will be smaller on this bigger card.
   d) Change the Layout of the Card:
      i) Choose one of 26 different layouts under **Layout** (lower right corner), click the little arrow
      ii) Try different **Layouts** until you find the one you like best
   e) Click **Create** when you're done
4) Change the verse options on the card:
   a) Click the **Page Design** tab on the **Ribbon**

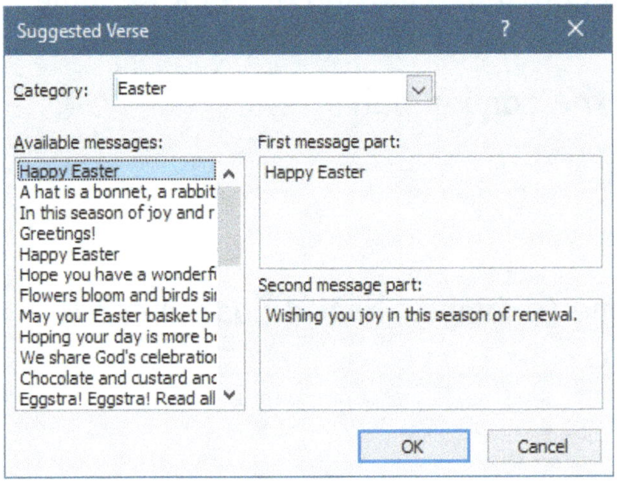

   b) In the **Template** group, click **Options**
   c) Click on the **Available Messages** on the right side to see what they say
   d) Click **OK** when you have chosen the one you want
   e) OR you can type whatever you want to say in the text boxes and change the words on all 4 sides of the card

5) To change sides of the card:
   a) Click the different pages in the **Pages** pane on the left side
6) Show that you created the card:
   a) Click on side 4 in the Page Navigation pane on the right
   b) Click in the text box below the text **Made especially for you by:**
   c) Select all the text in the box, then type your name in the box
7) Insert Online Pictures or your own Pictures:
   a) Click **Insert**
      i) Click **Online Pictures** (for online images)
      ii) or **Pictures** (to use a photo that you have on your computer)
8) When you have finished, print the card:
   a) These cards print best on card stock, but if you have none, paper will do fine.
   b) Insert only the one sheet of paper into the printer.
   c) Click **File**
   d) Click **Print**
   e) When the 1st side is done, flip the page over and re-insert the page into the printer to print side 2. **Make sure to follow your specific printer's directions here.**
   f) Press the button on the printer to continue printing or click Resume button if on screen
   g) When it's done printing, just fold the card in half.
9) To save the file:
   a) Click **File**
   b) Click **Save As**
   c) Type in Your name and project name (example: Nick's Easter card)
   d) Click **Save** button.

Lesson 24 Practice

Day 1

1. **Follow the steps to make another card for someone you know.**
2. **Print it out.**
3. **Give it to them and watch it brighten their day!**

Lesson Review:

1. What is a greeting card?

   ____

2. Which page size prints on BOTH sides of the paper?

   ____

3. Which card size fits in an invitation-size envelope?

   ____

Planning for our next lesson:

1. **Do you know what Microsoft PowerPoint does?**

   ____

2. **Have you ever used PowerPoint before?** Yes No

Lesson

25

25-A PowerPoint Presentation

Learn how to make a multimedia slide presentation showing how to make something!

About Our Project

We are going to make a slide presentation in PowerPoint to show how to fry an egg. Perhaps you know the steps on how to do that. If not, all the information is in the Step-by-Step. Here we go!

What you will learn

- What PowerPoint does
- What a slide show presentation is
- How to enter & delete text in PowerPoint
- How to add pictures, clipart & movies to slides
- How to rearrange slides in a presentation
- How to use presentation design templates
- How to run a slide show

What is a slide show presentation?

Slide show

The term **slide show** comes from an old-fashioned device called a **slide projector**. A slide projector shone a light beam through small negatives of photographs called **slides**, so they could be projected onto a screen or wall big enough for a room full of people to see, just like a movie projector.

35mm slide

This is a picture of a **35mm slide**, taken with a **35mm camera**. They were tiny! Only 2 inches x 2 inches with cardboard surrounding the picture negative.

Carousel slide projector

This is a picture of a **carousel slide projector**. Each carousel held from **80 to 120 slides**. To make a text slide, a large picture was drawn with all the information on it and a photo was taken of it. Then the photo was developed by a store and turned into a slide. Then the slides were loaded in order into the round tray. One by one, they would drop down in front of the light automatically and be projected for all to see. Imagine the work just to reorder the slides or to change one! Things are much simple now with presentation programs like Microsoft PowerPoint, as you will see.

Source: Wikimedia Commons, website: http://commons.wikimedia.org/wiki/File:Slide.jpg

Step-By-Step

Follow the steps below to create a slide presentation showing how to fry an egg.

1) <u>Open Microsoft PowerPoint:</u>
   a) In Windows 10, click the **Start** button OR in the Search box type **PowerPoint 2019**
   b) Click **PowerPoint 2019**
2) <u>Click on Blank presentation</u>
3) <u>Title your presentation:</u>
   a) Click in the box the says **Click to add title**
   b) Type in **How to Fry an Egg**
   c) Click in the box the says **Click to add subtitle**
   d) Type in **By: your name**

Title slide

4) <u>Add all your slides like an outline:</u> (we'll make them beautiful later!)
   a) On the **Ribbon**, on the **Home** tab, click the TOP PART of the **New Slide button** 4 times.
5) <u>Title all your slides</u> (you can change them later if you need to)
   a) Click on slide 2 on the left side to select it
   b) Click where it says **Click to add title**
   c) Type in **Get Items Needed**
   d) Click on slide 3 on the left side to select it
   e) Click where it says **Click to add title**
   f) Type in **Cook Egg**
   g) Click on slide 4 on the left side to select it
   h) Click where it says **Click to add title**
   i) Type in **Eat Egg**

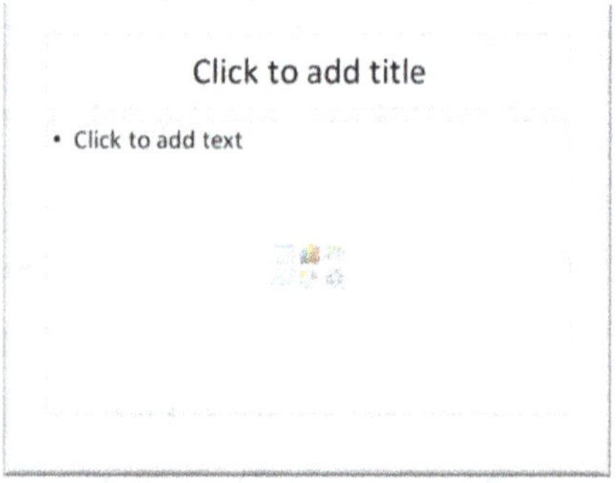

Title and Content slide

j) Click on slide 5 on the left side to select it
k) Click where it says **Click to add title**
l) Type in **Clean Up**

6) <u>Fill in the details for each slide:</u>
a) Click on slide 2 on the left side to select it
b) Click where it says **Click to add text**
c) Type in
i) Pan, press **Enter**
ii) Butter, press **Enter**
iii)Egg, press **Enter**
iv) Spatula, press **Enter**
v) Plate, press **Enter**
vi) Fork, press **Enter**
vii) Seasoning, press **Enter**

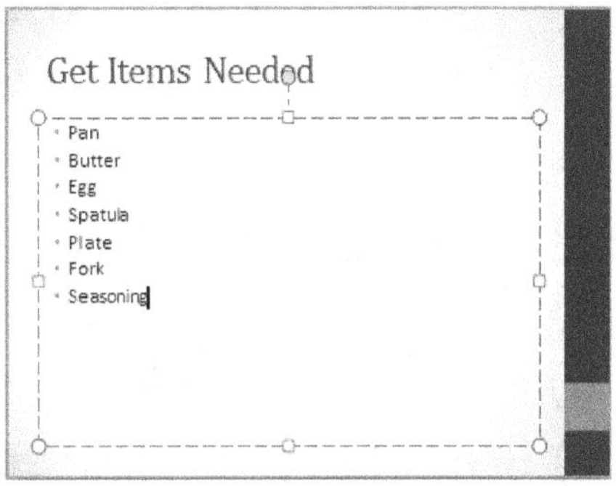

Be careful not to backspace or delete the bullets that are before the text. If you do, click the undo button at the top or press CTRL-Z.

d) Click on slide 3 on the left side to select it
e) Click where it says **Click to add text**
f) Type in
i) Put pan on stove, press **Enter**
ii) Turn stove on medium, press **Enter**
iii)Put butter in pan, press **Enter**
iv) Put egg into pan, press **Enter**
v) Flip egg if you like, press **Enter**
vi) Turn off stove, press **Enter**

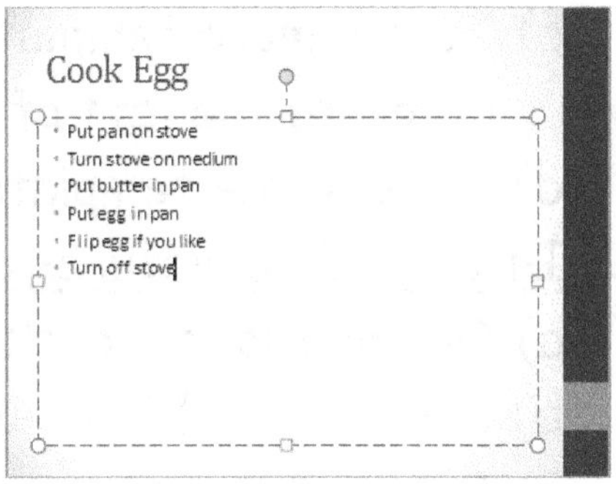

g) Click on slide 4 on the left side to select it
h) Click where it says **Click to add text**
i) Type in

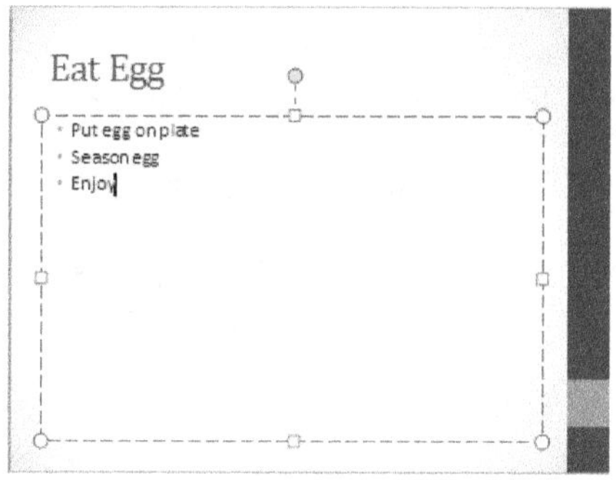

      i) Put egg on plate, press **Enter**
      ii) Season egg, press **Enter**
      iii) Enjoy, press **Enter**
   j) Click on slide 5 on the left side to select it
   k) Click where it says **Click to add text**
   l) Type in
      i) Wash dishes, press **Enter**
      ii) Dry dishes, press **Enter**
      iii) Put away dishes, press **Enter**

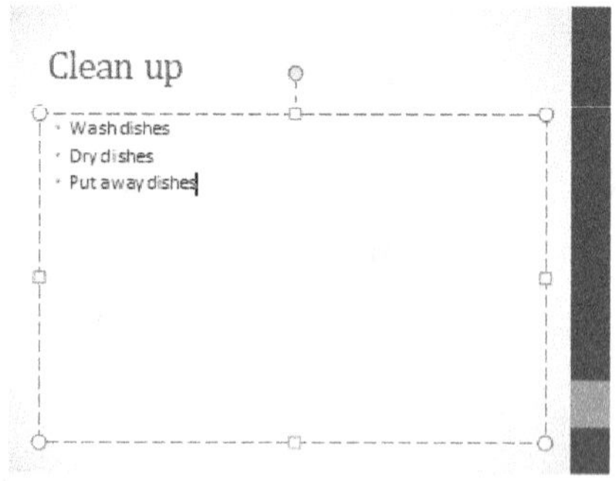

7) <u>Test your slide show presentation:</u>
   a) On the Ribbon, click **Slide Show**
   b) Click **From Beginning** (first button)
   c) Press **Enter** or **spacebar** or **click mouse** to go to next slides
   d) Click once more to **Exit** the presentation
8) <u>Now add apply a design template:</u>
   a) On the **Ribbon**, click the **Design** tab
   b) In the **Themes** group, slide over all the different themes and watch them as they preview on your slide
   c) To see more templates, click the **More** button, which is the little arrow to the left of **Effects**
   d) Click on the template you like best
9) <u>Insert online pictures & movies</u>
   a) On the Ribbon, click **Insert**
   b) Click **Online Pictures**
   c) Search for pictures for each slide: egg, pan, cook, butter, eat, fry, wash, clean, etc.
   d) Click each picture or video to add them to the presentation
   e) To insert videos, click Insert, Video, Online Video

Note: To see the videos run, you must add them to the slide and then RUN the slide show: Click Slide Show tab on Ribbon, click From Current Slide.

10) Test your slide show presentation:
    a) On the Ribbon, click **Slide Show**
    b) Click **From Beginning** (first button)
    c) Press **Enter** or **spacebar** or **click mouse** to go to next slides
    d) Click to **Exit** presentation
11) When you have finished, save the presentation:
    a) Click **File**
    b) Click **Save As**
    c) Type in Your name and project name (example: Nick's How to fry an egg).
    d) Click **Save** button
12) To print a page of small slides called Handouts:
    a) Click **File**
    b) Click **Print**
    c) Click arrow under **Slide**, change from **Full Page Slides** to **6 slides horizontal**
    d) Click **Print**

Lesson 25 Practice

Day 1

1. **Follow the steps to make another presentation.**
2. **Show it to your family and friends!**

Lesson Review:

1. What is PowerPoint used for?

2. How big were 35mm slides?

3. What do you click on to apply a design template with all the nice colors?

Planning for our next lesson:

1. **Think of a topic you would like to make a presentation on to the class. Choose a topic that you know a lot about: your favorite movies or video games, how to make something, how to play a certain sport, etc.**

   Presentation Title:

2. Write down 3 or 4 main points or steps you will tell about. Each one of these will be a separate slide in your presentation

Main point #1 or Step #1:

___

Main point #2 or Step #2:

___

Main point #3 or Step #3:

___

Main point #4 or Step #4:

___

3. Have in mind some of the details you will need to write after each main point on each slide. Make some notes below to help:

Notes for details:

___

___

___

4. Gather some images for your slide presentation and have them on your computer of flash drive for class.

You will make your presentation in class and then present it to the class.

Lesson

26

26-Presenting a Presentation

Now you that you know how to make your very own presentation and any topic you want, do it and then show it to everybody!

About Our Project

Now, use Microsoft PowerPoint to make your own slide show presentation. It can be about any topic you want: It can tell a story, describe someone or someplace, or show how to do something.

What you will learn

- How to make an outline for a presentation
- Review how to enter & delete text in PowerPoint
- Review how to add pictures
- Review how to rearrange slides
- Review how to use presentation design templates
- Review how to run a slide show
- Presentation skills

How to create a slide show presentation

When you design a slide show presentation, you need to:

1. Decide what topic or subject you will be using
2. Narrow down the topic for the time limit you have to give your presentation
3. Make an outline of the information you will present
4. Make slides to match each step in your outline
5. Practice giving your presentation
6. Give the presentation

How to give a slide show presentation

When your presentation is ready, here are a few tips to presenting it well:

- **Have plenty of slides for the time allowed.** In case you get nervous and talk fast, you don't want to finish your presentation way short of the time allowed.
- **Make sure you don't have too many slides, too.** If you end up going way over your allowed time, you may get cut off before you are finished.
- **Practice giving your presentation in front of someone.** This helps calm your nerves and helps you with your timing.
- Have fun with it!

Step-By-Step

Follow the steps below to create a PowerPoint presentation and then present it.

1) Open Microsoft PowerPoint:
   a) In Windows 10, click the **Start** button OR in the Search box type **PowerPoint 2019**
   b) Click **PowerPoint 2019**
   c) Click **Blank Presentation**
2) Choose a topic for your presentation. Pick something you know a lot about or how to do well.
3) Title your presentation:
   a) Click in the box the says **Click to add title**
   b) Type in the title of your presentation (you can always change it late if you want to)
   c) Click in the box the says **Click to add subtitle**
   d) Type in **By: your name**
4) Add all your slides like an outline: (we'll make them beautiful later!)
   a) On the **Ribbon**, on the **Home** tab, click the TOP PART of the **New Slide button** once for every slide you intend to have. This will automatically add the right slide layout you need.

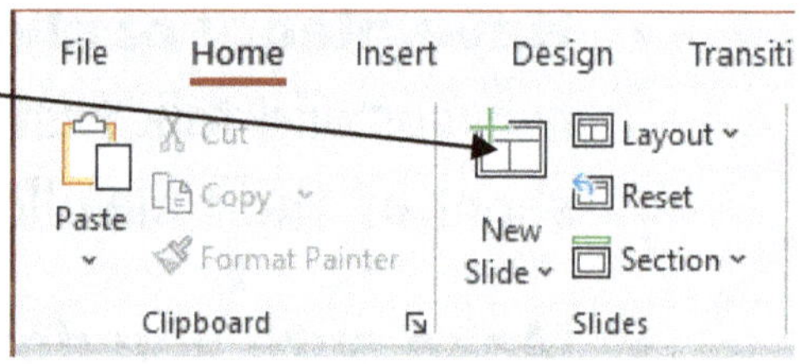

5) Title all your slides (you can change them later if you need to)
   a) Click on slide 2 on the left side to select it
   b) Click where it says **Click to add title**
   c) Type in your 1st main point from the outline you made for your presentation.
   d) Click on slide 3 on the left side to select it

e) Click where it says **Click to add title**
f) Type in your 2nd main point
g) Continue like this until you have entered a title on each slide

6) <u>Fill in the details for each slide:</u>
a) Click on slide 2 on the left side to select it

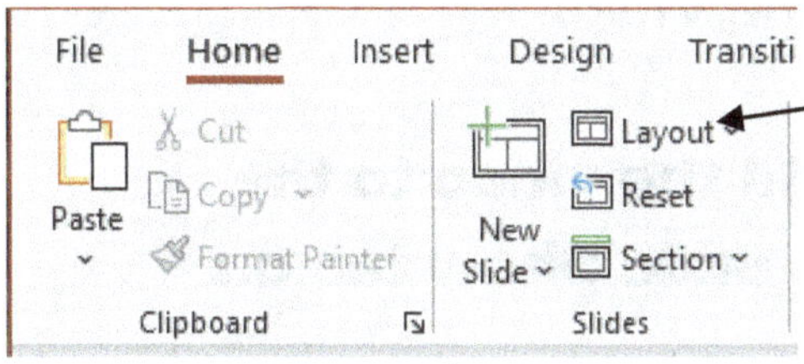

b) Is the layout right for this slide? You may want to change it with the **Layout** button first.
c) Now, add the information for the slide (words, pictures or both)
d) Continue like this until you have entered all the information on each slide

Be careful not to backspace or delete the bullets that are before the text. If you do, click the undo button at the top or press CTRL-Z.

7) <u>Test your slide show presentation:</u>
a) Click the **Slide Show** tab on the **Ribbon**
b) Click **From Beginning** button
c) Press **Enter** or **spacebar** or **click mouse** to go to next slides
d) Click to **Exit** presentation

8) <u>Now apply a design template for color and style:</u>
a) On the **Ribbon**, click the **Design** tab
b) In the **Themes** group, slide over all the different themes and watch them as they preview on your slide
c) To see more templates, click the **More** button, which is the little arrow to the left of **Effects**
d) Click on the template you like best
e) Try the **Variants** for the Theme you chose by clicking on them

9) Insert online pictures & movies
   a) On the Ribbon, click **Insert**
   b) Click **Online Pictures**
   c) Search for pictures for each slide: egg, pan, cook, butter, eat, fry, wash, clean, etc.
   d) Click each picture to add them to the presentation
   e) To insert videos, click Insert, Video, Online Video

Note: To see the video run, you must add the video to the slide and then run the slide show: Click Slide Show tab on Ribbon, click From Current Slide.

10) Test your slide show presentation:
   a) Click the **Slide Show** tab on the **Ribbon**
   b) Click **From Beginning** button
   c) Press **Enter** or **spacebar** or **click mouse** to go to next slides
   d) Click to **Exit** presentation

11) When you have finished, save the presentation:
   a) Click **File**
   b) Click **Save As**
   c) Type in Your name and project name (example: Nick's presentation).
   d) Click **Save** button

12) To print a page of small slides called Handouts:
   a) Click **File**
   b) Click **Print**
   c) Click arrow under **Slides**, change to **Full Page Slides** to **3 Slides or 6 or 9 slides**
   d) Click **Print**

13) Present the presentation to the class!

Lesson 26 Practice

Day 1

1. **Create another presentation in PowerPoint to show your family.**
2. **Print out the slides in Handout form.**
3. **Put the printout in your binder with the other projects from this year.**

Lesson Review:

1. What could a PowerPoint presentation be used for?

    ____

2. Can you insert a video into a presentation?

    ____

3. How many slides can you PRINT on a page?

    ____

Planning for our next lesson:

1. **Think of business for which you would like to make a set of business cards. This can be your OWN business, a family business or a friend's business. If there is not a real business that you can use, simply make up a business!**

   Business Name: ______________________________

2. **Write down the address of the business:**

   Street Address:

   ____

   City: ______________ State:_____ Zip: _______

3. **Find a logo or small picture for your business cards**. Load it onto your flash drive or computer.

Lesson

27

27-Making Business Cards in Publisher

Real business cards for your own business or for someone else!

About Our Project

We are going to make business cards in Publisher. You can make them in Word, but it's not as easy and you have to customize each one if you want a picture on them. It's much easier in Publisher because you can work on one card in full screen and then it makes all the copies. Let's get to it!

What you will learn

- What a business card is
- How to use a business card template in Publisher

What is a business card?

A business card is a small rectangle of card stock with a business's name, address, phone number, fax number, website, email address, sometimes a map, pictures and other information that will help anyone be able to contact that business. It helps get clients and sales and increases your business.

Many kids and families have their own small businesses making things and selling them, providing services for people or volunteering for others. Also, many homeschool families have their own businesses. So, custom made business cards are very helpful to advertise those businesses.

Making your own business cards is fast and easy. The cards are easy to update and make changes to. You can make as many or as few as you need whenever you need them.

Let's get started!

Step-By-Step

Follow the steps below to create your own business cards in Microsoft Publisher.

1) Open Microsoft Publisher 2019:
    a) In Windows 10, click the **Start button** **OR in the** Search box type **Publisher 2019**
    b) Click **Publisher 2019**
2) Choose your business card template:
    a) Click **BUILT-IN**
    b) Click on **Business Cards**
    c) Click ONCE on the business card that you want
3) In the right pane, **Customize** the business card the way you want it:
    a) Change the Color scheme

        i) Click **Color Scheme** on right side
        ii) Click a color scheme you like. Try as many as you like, only the last choice stays.
    b) <u>Change the Font scheme</u>
        i) Click **Font Scheme** on right side
        ii) Click a font scheme you like. Try as many as you like, only the last choice stays.
    c) <u>Change the Layout of the Card:</u>
        i) Choose one **Landscape** (most common) or **Portrait**.
    d) Click **Create** on the bottom right side when you're done
4) <u>Change the information on the card:</u>
    a) Select **Business Name** and type in your name
    b) Select **Title** and type in what you do like Artist, Painter, Designer, Lawn Care Specialist, etc.
    c) Change the **Primary Business Address lines** to show YOUR businesses address, email & phone number
5) <u>Insert a picture to replace the Organization logo:</u>
    a) Click on the Organization Logo and press the Delete key on your keyboard
    b) Click **Insert**
        i) Click **Online Pictures** (for online images)
        ii) or **Pictures** (to use a photo you have taken)
    c) Search for the image you want and click on it to insert it
6) <u>When you have finished, print the cards:</u>
    a) These cards print best on special business card paper, but if you have none, card stock will do.
    b) It is best to test printing on a sheet of paper first to make sure the cards will fit on the business card paper.
        i) Insert only one sheet of paper into the printer.
        ii) Click **File**

iii) Click **Print**
iv) Click **Print**

c) Hold up the printed paper to the business cards to a light. You should be able to see if the card text will fit well on each card. If not, you may have to adjust the margins of the cards.

d) Once it fits fine, print the cards on the business card paper.

i) Insert only the one sheet of business card paper into the printer.
ii) Click **File**
iii) Click **Print**
iv) Click **Print**

e) Separate the cards, of if on card stock, cut into rectangles.

7) <u>To save the file:</u>

a) Click **File**
b) Click **Save As**
c) Type in Your name and project name (example: Nick's business card)
d) Click **Save** button.

Lesson 27 Practice

Day 1

1. Follow the steps to make another set of business cards for a family member or a friend.

2. Print them out.

3. And give them.

Lesson Review:

1. What is a business card?

   ____

2. What does clicking on Color Scheme do?

   ____

3. What does clicking on Font Scheme do?

   ____

Planning for our next lesson:

1. **For the business that you made the business cards for, we will make a budget.**

   Business Name: ________________________________

2. **How will your business make money?** Will you sell things? Will you provide a service (do things for people)?

   ____

3. **What might you have to BUY to run your business?**

   ____

Lesson

28

28-Make a Business Budget in Excel

A nice form to keep track of business expenses and profit!

About Our Project

This time we are going to make a business budget in Excel to keep track of business expenses and our net profit.

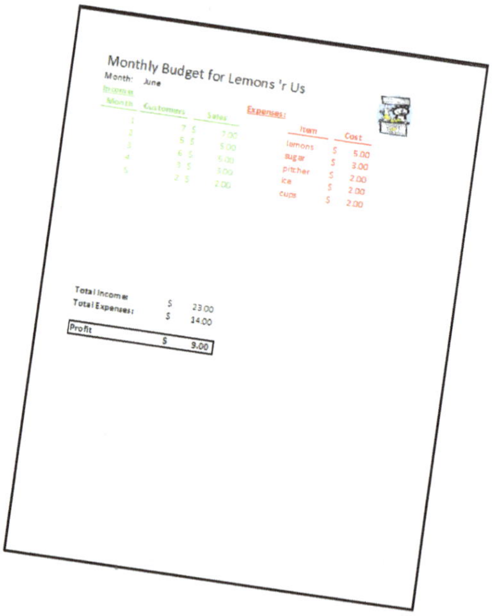

What you will learn

- What a business budget is
- What income is
- What expenses are
- What profit is
- Review how to add & subtract in Excel
- Review how to write a formula in Excel
- Review how to use a function in Excel

Step-By-Step

Follow the steps below to create a monthly business budget in Microsoft Excel.

1) Open Microsoft Excel 2019:
   a) In Windows 10, click the **Start button** **OR in the** Search box type **Excel 2019**
   b) Click **Excel 2019**
2) Click **Blank workbook**
3) Set the font size bigger so it's easier to read and see:
   a) Click on the **Select All** button before the column A heading and above the row 1 heading.
   b) On the **Ribbon**, on the **Home** tab, in the **Font** group, increase the font size to 14.

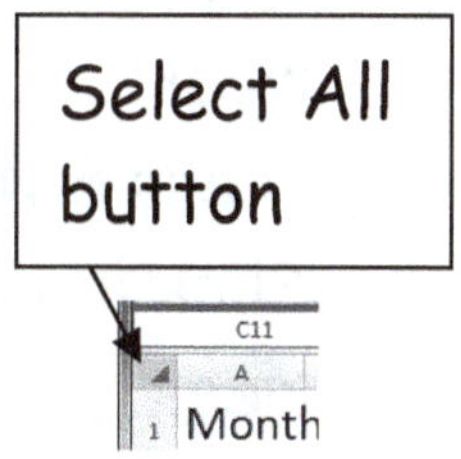

4) Title your budget:
   a) In cell A1 type **Monthly Budget for (type your company name)**
   b) Press **Enter**
5) Add the month name that the budget will cover:
   a) In cell A2, type **Month:**
   b) Press **TAB**
   c) In cell B2 type the upcoming month name (November, December, January, etc.)
   d) Press **TAB**
6) Now let's enter the major column headings:
   a) Click on cell A3 and type **Income:**
   b) Press **TAB** 4 times on your keyboard to move to cell E3
   c) Type in **Expenses:**
   d) Press **Enter**
7) Now let's enter the minor column headings:
   a) Click on cell A4 and type **Week #**

b) Press **TAB** on your keyboard to move to cell B4.
c) Type **Customers**
d) Press **TAB** on your keyboard to move to cell C4.
e) Type **Sales**
f) Press **TAB** twice to move to cell E4. Type **Item**
g) Press **TAB** to move to cell F4. Type **Cost**
h) Press **Enter**

8) Let's enter the numbers of the weeks we are tracking:
   a) Click in cell A5 and type a 1 for the first week.
   b) Press **Enter**
   c) Click in cell A6 and type a 2 for the second week.
   d) Press **Enter**
   e) Select both cells A5 and A6
   f) Click on the **Fill Handle** and pull down 3 rows.
   This will enter in the next 3 week-numbers for us to complete the month with 5 weeks. (Some months have 4 weeks, some have 5. For those months with only 4 weeks, we'll just leave week 5 blank.)

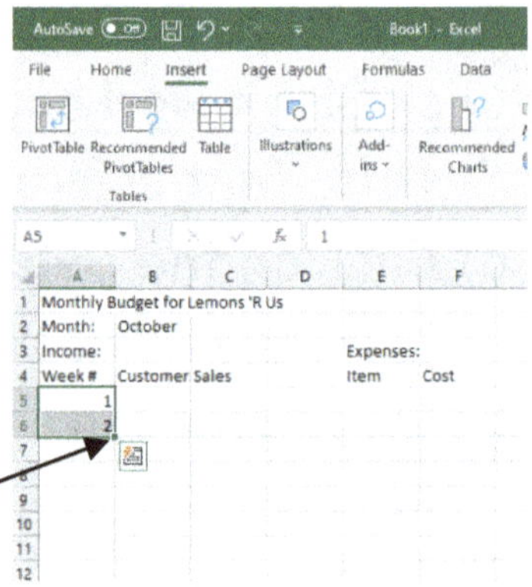

9) Now, to enter your income:
   a) First enter in the number of customers you expect per week:
      i) Click on cell B5 and type in the number of customers you will have during the 1st week of the month and press **Enter**.
      ii) In cell B6, type in the number of customers you will have during the 2nd week of the month and press **Enter**.
      iii) Now, in cell B7, type in the number of customers you will have during the 3rd week of the month and press **Enter**.
      iv) Now, in cell B8, type in the number of customers you will have during the 4th week of the month and press **Enter**.

v) In cell B9, type in the number of customers you will have during the 5th week of the month (if there was a fifth week, otherwise leave it blank) and press **Enter**.

b) Next enter a formula to calculate the amount of sales dollars:

i) Click on cell C5 and type in an = sign.

ii) Click on cell B5 (this will enter the number of customers you had the 1st week).

iii) Press the * key (Shift-8) for the multiply sign.

iv) Now type in the cost of one item (here it's a cup of lemonade), without dollar signs.

v) Press **Enter**.

vi) Now, we'll copy the formula down so we don't have to keep retyping it:

(1) Click on cell C5.

(2) Grab the **Fill Handle** and pull down 4 rows. Isn't that awesome?

10) Let's add dollar signs for our money columns:

a) Click on the column heading for column C (click right on it) to select the whole column.

b) Click the **$** on the **Ribbon**, on the **Home** tab in the **Number** group.

c) Click on the column heading for column F (click right on it) to select the whole column.

d) Click the **$** on the **Ribbon**, on the **Home** tab in the **Number** group.

11) Now, to enter our expenses:

a) Click on cell E5 and type in the 1st expense of the month (in this case, lemons) and press **TAB** to move to the Cost column and enter in the cost of that item.

b) Press **Enter**

c) Click on cell E6 and type in the 2nd expense of the month (in this case, sugar) and press **TAB** to move to the Cost column and enter in the cost of that item.

d) Press **Enter**

e) Click on cell E7 and type in the 3rd expense of the month (in this case, pitcher) and press **TAB** to move to the Cost column and enter in the cost of that item.

f) Press **Enter**

g) Click on cell E8 and type in the 4th expense of the month (in this case, ice) and press **TAB** to move to the Cost column and enter in the cost of that item.

h) Press **Enter**

i) Click on cell E9 and type in the 5th expense of the month (in this case, cups) and press **TAB** to move to the Cost column and enter in the cost of that item.

j) Continue in this way until all the Expenses are entered.

12) <u>Now we need to find the totals of our income and expenses:</u>

a) Click in cell A19 and type **Total Income**.

b) Press **TAB** twice.

c) In cell C19, click on the **Σ AutoSum** button on the **Ribbon**, on the **Home** tab in the **Editing** Group.

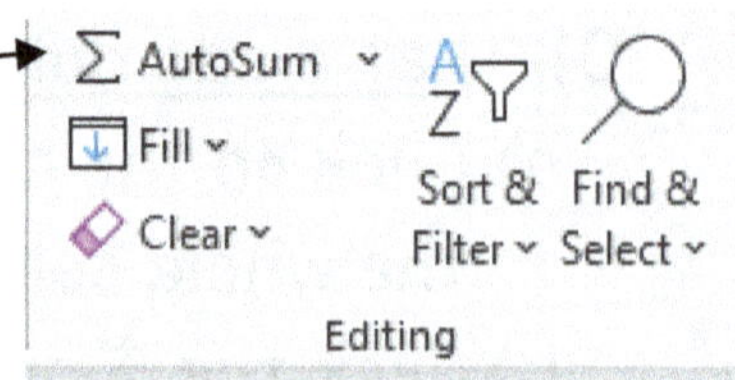

d) Press **Enter**. Excel added up all the money you made!

e) Click in cell A20 and type **Total Expenses**.

f) Press **TAB** twice.

g) In cell C20, click on the **Σ AutoSum** button on the **Ribbon**, on the **Home** tab in the **Editing** Group.

h) Drag over all the Cost numbers (cells F5-F17 or as far down as they go).

i) Press **Enter**. Excel added up all the costs for you!

13) <u>Now, to calculate our Profit:</u>

a) Click in Cell A21 and type **Profit**.

b) Press **TAB** twice.

c) Type and = sign.
d) Click on the number for your total income (cell C19 in this example).
e) Type a – sign to subtract.
f) Click on the number for your total expenses (C20 in this example).
g) Press **Enter**.

14) Now, if you need to widen the columns:
a) Hover your mouse between the column heading letters A and B. You should see a two-headed black arrow. Click and drag to the right until it is 73 pixels wide.
b) Hover your mouse between the column heading letters B and C. You should see a two-headed black arrow. Double-click and it will automatically resize the column to as wide as you need.
c) Repeat this process between each of the column headings until everything fits and you no longer see any cells with ##### in them.

15) Let's center the column headings and bold & underline them:
a) Click right on the row number 3 to select the whole row, hold the mouse button down and select row 4, too.
b) Click the **Center** button on the **Ribbon** in the **Alignment** Group.
c) Click the **Bold** button on the **Ribbon** in the **Font** group.
d) Click the **Underline** button on the **Ribbon** in the **Font** group.

16) Now take a look in Print Preview
a) Click the **File**, then **Print**
b) Click the **File** again to close **Print Preview**
c) Now, make sure you don't add anything past the black dotted line on the right side or below, or your budget will not fit on one page.

17) Now to make the title nicer:
a) Click on A1.
b) Change the font style and size (22 is a good title size font).

18) Insert a small picture of something that represents your business in the upper left corner.

a) Click the **Insert** tab on the **Ribbon**
b) Click **Online Pictures** in the **Illustrations** group on the **Ribbon**

19) Let's make the expenses font red and the income font green.
a) Select all the words and numbers for the income area (A3-C17).
b) Select the tiny arrow next to the **Font Color** button (on the **Ribbon**, on the **Home** tab, in the **Font** group)
c) Click on a green color.
d) Select all the words and numbers for the expenses area (E3-F17).
e) Select the tiny arrow next to the **Font Color** button (on the **Ribbon**, on the **Home** tab, in the **Font** group)
f) Click on a red color.

20) Put a box around the profit line:
a) Select cells A21-C21.
b) Click the tiny arrow next to the **Borders** button in the **Font** group on the **Home** tab on the **Ribbon**.
c) Click on **Thick Outside Borders**.

21) When you have finished, print the form:
a) Click **File**
b) Click **Print**
c) Click **Print**

22) To save the file:
a) Click **File**
b) Click **Save As**
c) Type in Your name and project name (example: Nick's Business Budget).
d) Click **Save** button

Lesson 28 Practice

Day 1

1. Follow the steps to make another budget for spending and saving in another business.

2. Print it out.

Lesson Review:

1. What is a budget?

____

2. How do you find your business' profit?

____

3. What is an expense?

____

Planning for our next lesson:

1. **Do you have any special events coming up like someone's birthday, an anniversary, a graduation or something else?**

____

2. **Are you planning on selling some things soon?**

_______________ _______________ _______________

Lesson

29

29-Banners & Flyers in Publisher

You can make a banners & flyers in just minutes!

About Our Project

We are going to make a banner and a flyer to advertise some events in Microsoft Publisher quickly and easily.

What you will learn

- What a banner is
- What a flyer is
- How to use banner templates in Publisher
- How to use flyer templates in Publisher

What is a banner?

A long strip of cloth or paper that has a slogan or designs on it that is hung in a public place or carried in a demonstration or procession. These are fun to make to celebrate people's birthdays or homecomings from trips. Here is an example:

What is a flyer?

A flyer is an advertisement (usually printed on a page or in a leaflet) intended for wide distribution. They can have strips along the bottom that you can tear off with a contact person's name and phone number on them. They can announce sales of items, events and more!

Let's get started!

Step-By-Step

Follow the steps below to create a banner in Microsoft Publisher.

1) Open Microsoft Publisher 2019:
   a) In Windows 10, click the **Start button** **OR in the** Search box type **Publisher 2019**
   b) Click **Publisher 2019**
2) Choose your template:
   a) Click **BUILT-IN**
   b) Click on **Banners**
   c) Click ONCE on the banner style that you want
3) In the right pane, Customize the banner the way you want it:
   a) Change the Color scheme
      i) Click **Color Scheme** on right side (some templates are not changed by this option)
      ii) Click a color scheme you like. Try as many as you like, only the last choice stays.
   b) Change the Font scheme
      i) Click **Font Scheme** on right side
      ii) Click a font scheme you like. Try as many as you like, only the last choice stays.
   c) Change Page Size, if you want to:
      i) For this class choose **5 ft. x 8.5 in**
   d) Change the border, if you want to:
      i) Choose **Border** or **No border**
   e) Change the graphic placement, if you want to:
      i) Choices are **Both**, **Left**, **Right** or **None**
   f) Click **Create** when you're done
4) Enter the information for the banner:

   a) Click on the banner and type in the text you want on it

5) Insert Online Pictures:
   a) Click **Insert**
   b) Click **Online Pictures**
   c) Click on the picture you want
   d) Click **Insert**

6) When you have finished, print the banner:
   a) Click **File**
   b) Click **Print**
   c) Click **Print**
   d) When it's done printing, just tape all the banner pages together.

7) To save the banner:
   a) Click **File**
   b) Click **Save As**
   c) Type in Your name and project name (example: Nick's banner)
   d) Click **Save** button

Now, we will make a flyer in Word. Let's get started!

Step-By-Step

Follow the steps below to create a flyer with tabs in Microsoft Publisher.

1) Open Microsoft Publisher:
   a) In Windows 10, click the **Start button** **OR in the** Search box type **Publisher 2019**
   b) Click **Publisher 2019**

2) Choose your template:
   a) Click **BUILT-IN**
   b) Click once on **Flyers**

   c) Click on the **All Event** yellow folder on the far right side on the first row
   d) Scroll down the **Installed Templates** section
   e) Scroll down and look through the available templates
   f) Click ONCE on the flyer style that you want
3) <u>In the right pane, customize the flyer the way you want it:</u>
   a) <u>Change the Color scheme</u>
      i) Click **Color Scheme** on right side (some templates are not changed by this option)
      ii) Click a color scheme you like. Try as many as you like, only the last choice stays.
   b) <u>Change the Font scheme</u>
      i) Click **Font Scheme** on right side
      ii) Click a font scheme you like. Try as many as you like, only the last choice stays.
   c) <u>Under the Options section:</u>
      i) Check **Include graphic**
      ii) Under the **Tear-offs** section, click the arrow
      iii) Click on **Contact Information** (notice all the other fun options, too!)

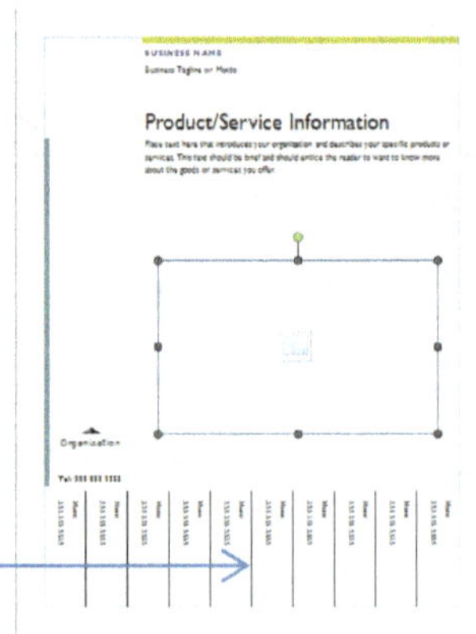

   d) Click **Create** when you're done
4) <u>Enter the information for the flyer:</u>
   a) Click on the flyer title and type in the title of your flyer
   b) Click in the text boxes and type in the information for your flyer
5) <u>To add a big picture:</u>
   a) Hover your mouse over the big, white area in the middle of your flyer
   b) When you see the **mountains & sun picture**, click once
   c) Now click on the mountain & sun picture and a window will open up to find your picture on your computer or flash drive

   d) When you find your picture you want, double-click it (it will be place inside the picture box and fitted for you automatically)

6) Type in the information on the tabs – you only have to type one:
   a) Click on the first tab
   b) All the text will be highlighted
   c) Just start typing your name
   d) Press **Enter**
   e) Then type in your phone number
   f) Click anywhere else on your flyer and all the other tabs will be filled in the same way!
7) Insert more Online Pictures or Pictures
   a) Click **Insert**
   b) Click **Online Pictures,** choose the picture you want, click **Insert**
   c) Or **Insert, Pictures** (to use a photo you have taken)
8) When you have finished, print the flyer:
   a) Click **File**
   b) Click **Print**
   c) Click **Print**
   d) When it's done printing, use a scissors to snip along the dotted line to loosen the tabs. Be careful not to cut them off!
9) To save the flyer:
   a) Click **File**
   b) Click **Save As**
   c) Type in Your name and project name (example: Nick's flyer)
   d) Click **Save** button

Lesson 29 Practice

Day 1

1. Follow the steps to make another banner or flyer for someone you know.

2. Hang it up for them and watch them smile!

Lesson Review:

1. What is a banner?

2. What is a flyer?

3. Why would you add tear-offs to the flyer?

Planning for our next lesson:

1. **We are making a Weekly Homework Chart so list all the subjects you have to do for school:**

Subject: ______________________________

Subject: ______________________________

Subject: ______________________________

Subject: ______________________________

Subject: ______________________________

Subject: ______________________________

Subject: ______________________________

Subject: ______________________________

Lesson

30

30-Weekly Homework Chart in Excel

A useful chart to help track the homework you need to do or see what FREE TIME you really have!

About Our Project

Today we are going to create a chart to track the homework that we need to do each week.

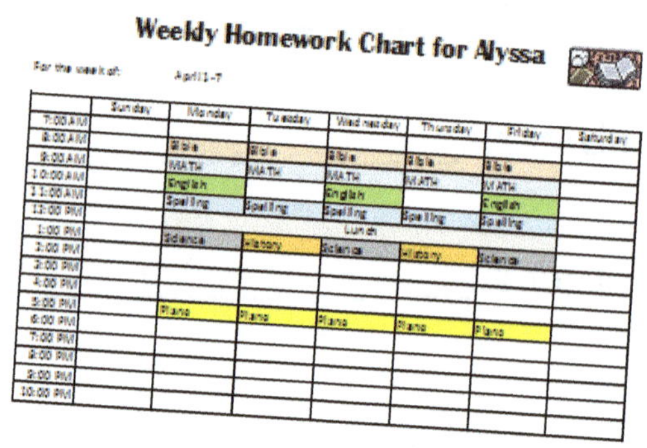

What you will learn

- What a homework chart is
- Review using Excel
- Review the fill handle
- Learn how to fill cells with color

What is a homework chart?

This is a chart that will **help us track what it is we need to do** so we can get it done and **have more free time** to do things we love! A chart like this also is wonderful to look back at each week to **see how much we have accomplished** through the school year!

Weekly Homework Chart for Alyssa

For the week of: April 1-7

	Sunday	Monday	Tuesday	Wednesday	Thursday	Friday	Saturday
7:00 AM							
8:00 AM		Bible	Bible	Bible	Bible	Bible	
9:00 AM		MATH	MATH	MATH	MATH	MATH	
10:00 AM		English		English		English	
11:00 AM		Spelling	Spelling	Spelling	Spelling	Spelling	
12:00 PM				Lunch			
1:00 PM		Science	History	Science	History	Science	
2:00 PM							
3:00 PM							
4:00 PM							
5:00 PM		Piano	Piano	Piano	Piano	Piano	
6:00 PM							
7:00 PM							
8:00 PM							
9:00 PM							
10:00 PM							

Step-By-Step

Follow the steps below to create a Weekly Homework Chart in Excel.

1) Open Microsoft Excel 2019:
   a) In Windows 10, click the **Start button** **OR in the** Search box type **Excel 2019**
   b) Click **Excel 2019**
2) Click **Blank workbook**
3) Title the chart:
   a) Click on the very first cell A1
   b) Type **Weekly Homework Chart for (type your name)**
   c) Press **Enter**
4) Now let's enter the date range:
   a) Click on cell A2 and type **For the week of:**
   b) Press **TAB** twice on your keyboard to move to cell C2.
   c) Type the dates this chart will cover. For Example: **April 1-7**.
   d) Press **TAB** to move to cell C3.
5) Now let's enter the column headings:
   a) Click on cell B5 and type Sunday
   b) Press **Enter**
   c) Click back on the word Sunday (on cell B5)
   d) Now hover your mouse over the **Fill Handle** in the lower right corner of the cell, and drag it to the right until it says Saturday. Then let go.

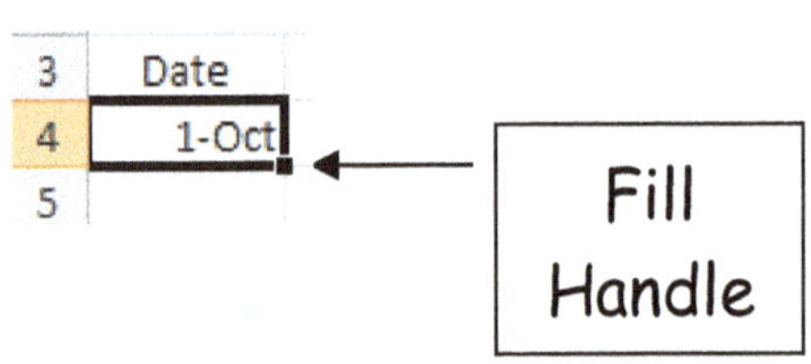

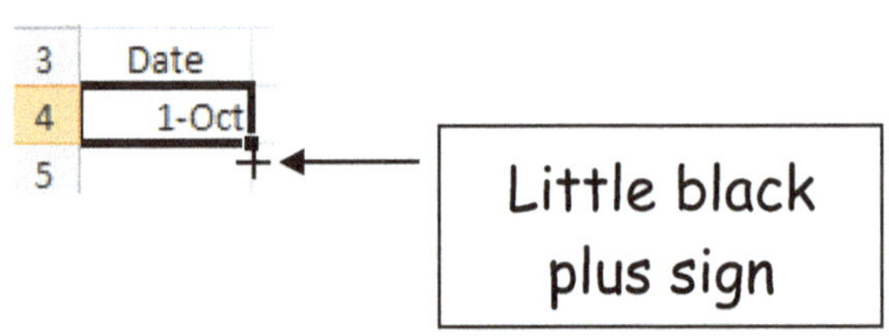

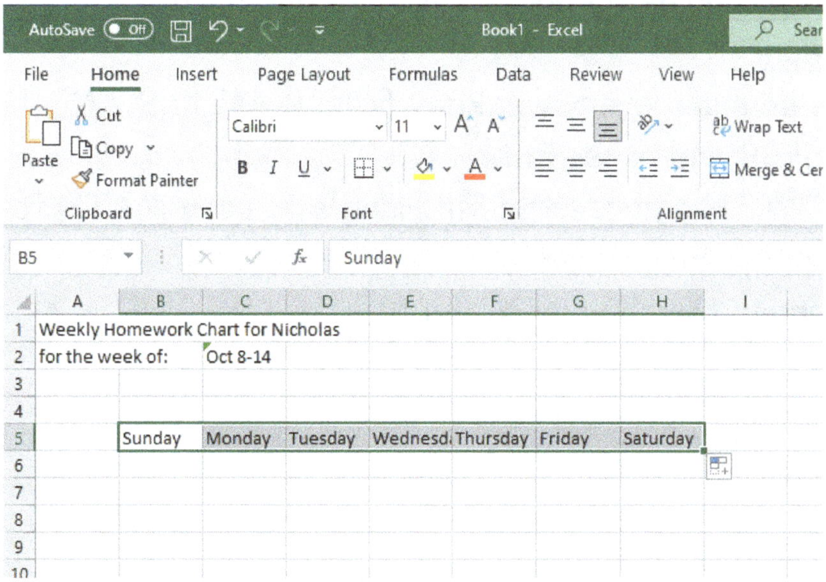

Don't worry how thin the columns are right now. We'll fix that later.

6) <u>Enter the row headings:</u>
   a) Click in A6 and type 7 am (or earlier if your days start earlier). Make sure there is one space between the "7" and the "am".
   b) Press **Enter** and it will change automatically to 7:00 AM
   c) Click back on the 7:00 AM (on cell A6)
   d) Now hover your mouse over the **Fill Handle** in the lower right corner and drag it down until it says 10:00 PM. Then let go.

7) <u>Now, to widen the columns:</u>
   a) Select columns B thru H by clicking right on top of the B and click and drag to the H.
   b) Hover your mouse between the column heading letters B and C. You should see a two-headed black arrow.
   c) Click and hold the mouse button down and drag it to the left until it reads (81 pixels) wide. That should be wide enough.

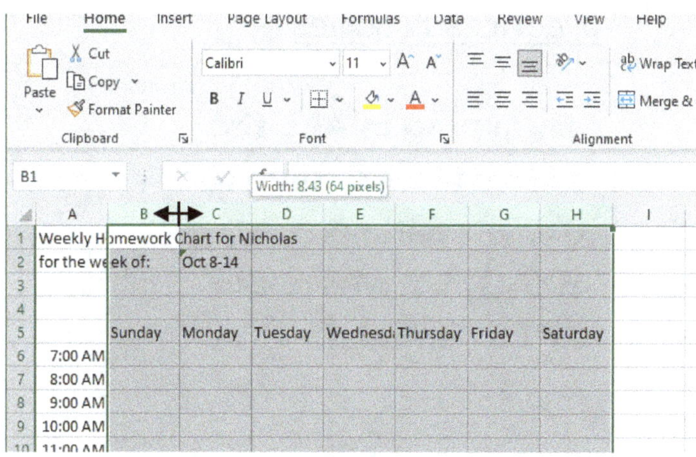

8) Type in the subjects & assignments under the days and across from the times they are to be done:

a) For example, if you do math every weekday from 8 AM to 9 AM, then type MATH into cell C8 and press **Enter**.

b) Then click back on MATH and use the Fill Handle to copy MATH to the right in cells D8, E8, F8 and G8.

c) Continue in that manner for all your subjects.

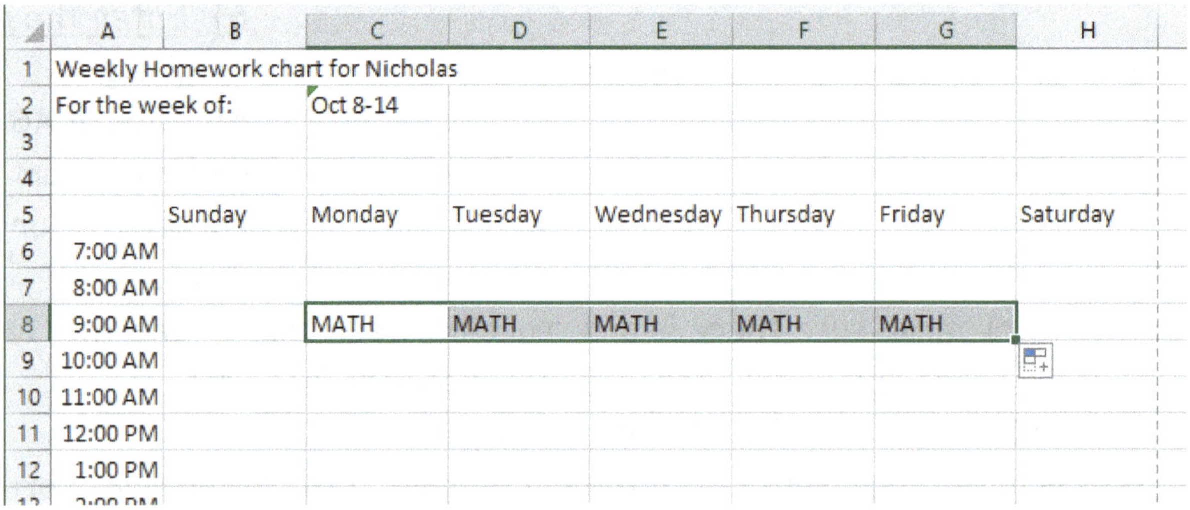

9) Now type in any activities you have outside school time, like music lessons or sports practices in games

By typing in ALL the activities we have to do, we can see EXACTLY where our FREE TIME is!

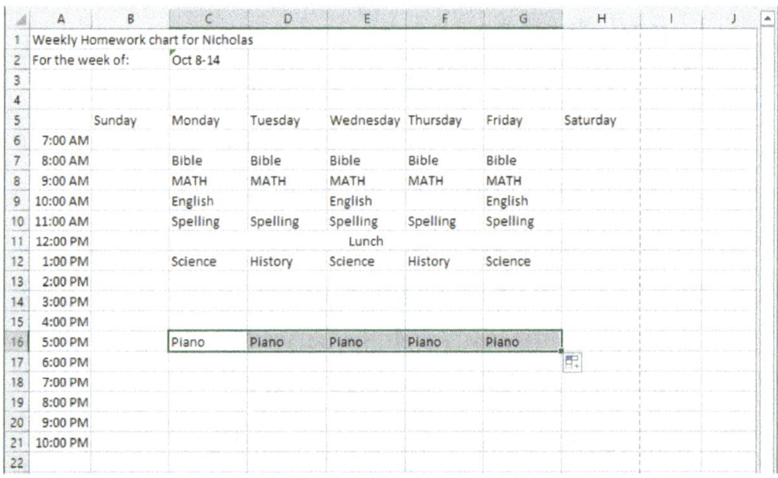

10) Let's center the column headings:

a) Click right on the row number **5** to select the whole row. It will become shaded.

e) Click the **Center** button on the **Ribbon** in the **Alignment** group.

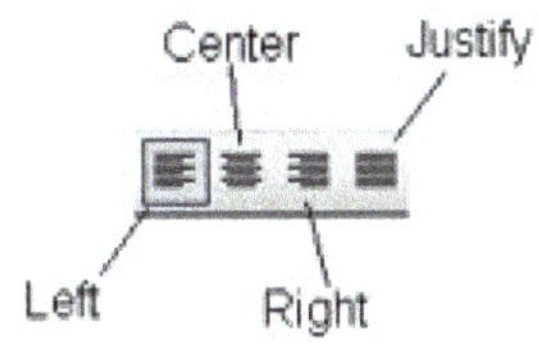

Text Alignment buttons

11) Now take a look in Print Preview:

a) Click the **File**, then **Print**

12) What's missing? The **Borders**! Let's add them:

a) Select all your rows and columns of your Weekly Homework Chart:

i) Click on cell A5, holding down your mouse button, drag over to cell H5 and continue downward till you reach the last row starting with 10:00 PM. Let go of the mouse button.

b) On the **Ribbon**, in the **Font** group, look for the **Bottom Border** button. Click the tiny, black arrow next to the box for choices.

c) Click on **All Borders**.

d) Now click on **File, Print** again to see what it looks like.

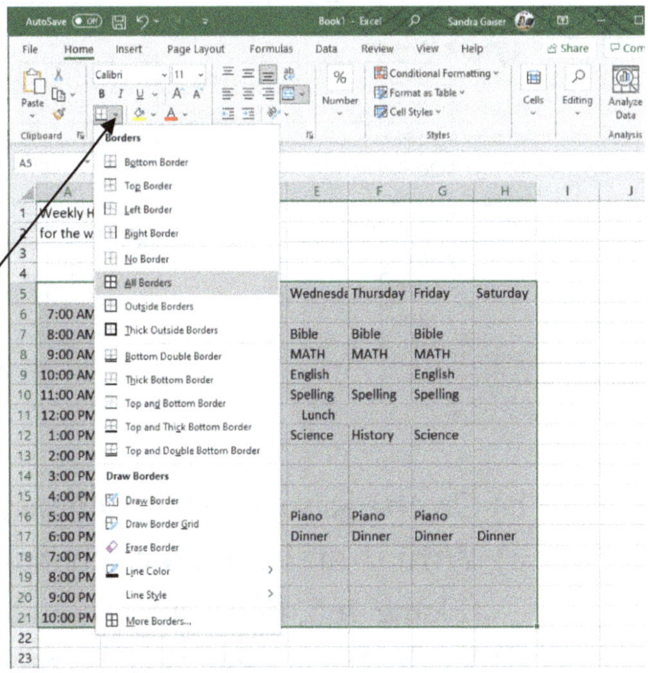

13) Now to make the title look nicer:

a) Click in the middle of cell A1 and drag (with the white plus sign) over to H1 to select the top row of the first page.

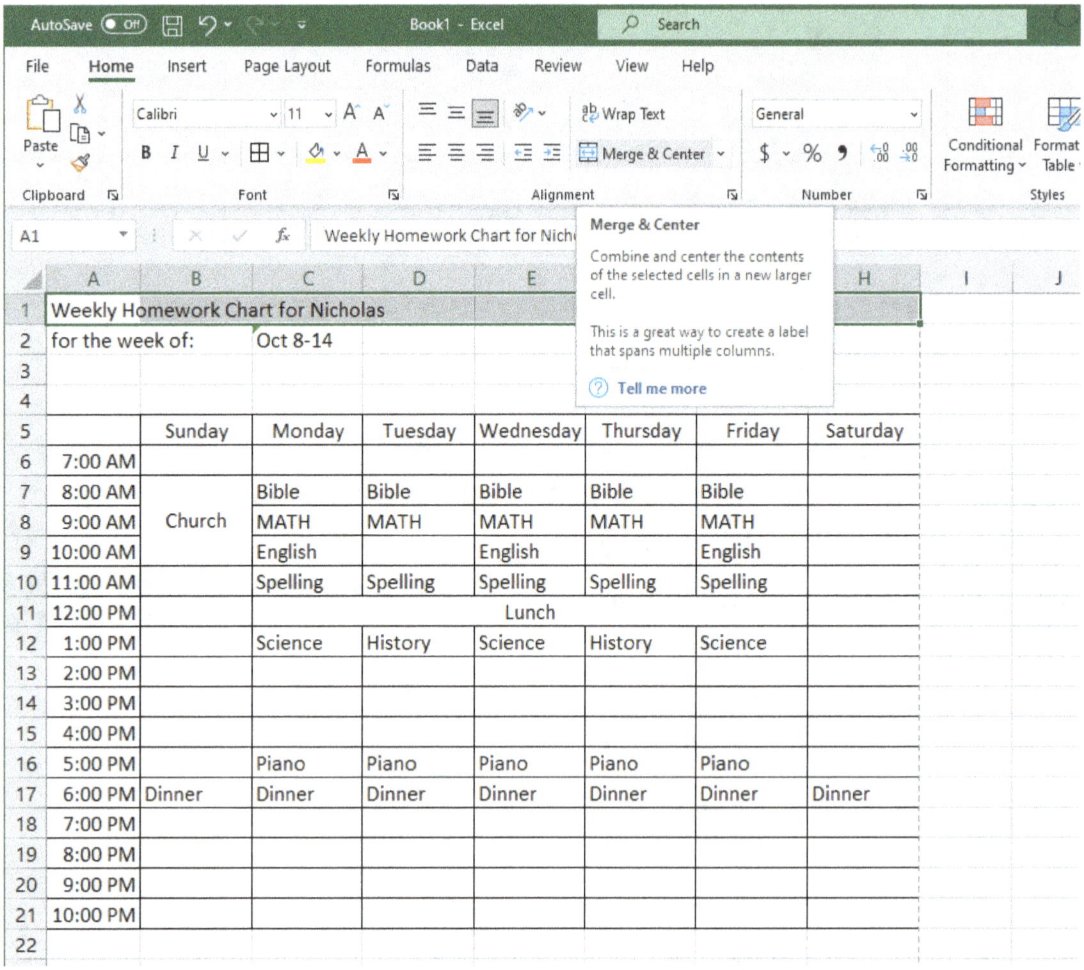

b) On the **Ribbon**, in the **Alignment Group**, click **Merge and Center**.

c) With it still selected, change the font style to something you like: (**Home** tab, **Font** group)

d) With it still selected, increase the size (**Home** tab, **Font** group) (22 is a good title size font).

e) With it still selected, change the **Font Color** to your favorite color.

14) <u>Insert a small picture of homework in the upper right corner:</u>
   a) Click the **Insert** tab on the **Ribbon**.
   b) Click the **Online Pictures** button in the **Illustrations** group.
   c) Grab the white corners & shrink it down so it fits.

15) <u>Color in the subject boxes for fun:</u>
   a) Select all the MATH cells using the white plus sign.
   b) Click on the little black arrow to the right of **Font Color** (the **paint can** in the **Font** group) in the **Home** tab of the **Ribbon**.
   c) Pick a color that you like or that matches your textbook for MATH.
   d) Continue like this until you have colored all the subjects like you want them.

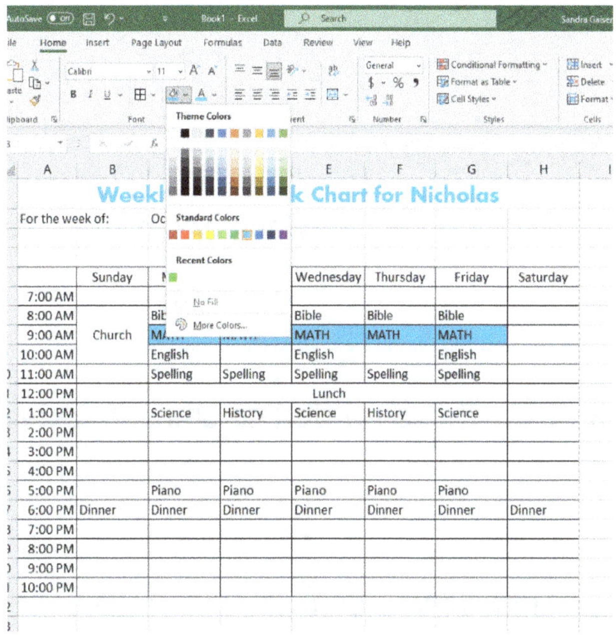

16) <u>When you have finished, print the form:</u>
   a) Click **File**
   b) Click **Print**
   c) Click **Print**

17) <u>To save the file:</u>
   a) Click **File**
   b) Click **Save As**
   c) Choose where you want to save your file
   d) Type in Your name & project name (example: Nick's Homework chart).
   e) Click **Save** button

Lesson 30 Practice

Day 1

1. **Show one of your friends how to make a homework chart!**

Lesson Review:

1. What is a homework chart used for?

2. How do you widen columns in Excel?

3. How do you center text in Excel?

Planning for our next lesson:

1. **We are making a newsletter so choose what kind of newsletter you want to write:**

   A school newsletter? A sport newsletter? A holiday newsletter? A family newsletter?

2. **Think of 1 main story you want to write about for the front page:**

   Main story is about: ____

3. **Think of 2-3 smaller stories you want to write about:**

   1st small story is about:

   ____

   2nd small story is about:

   ____

   3rd small story is about:

   ____

4. **Gather some pictures on your computer or flash drive for your news stories.**

Lesson
31

31-Make a Newsletter in Publisher

Learn how to make a newsletter for your school, club, or your family!

About Our Project

A newsletter is just that: **a letter that presents the news**! Microsoft Publisher has easy to use templates that are already formatted.

What you will learn

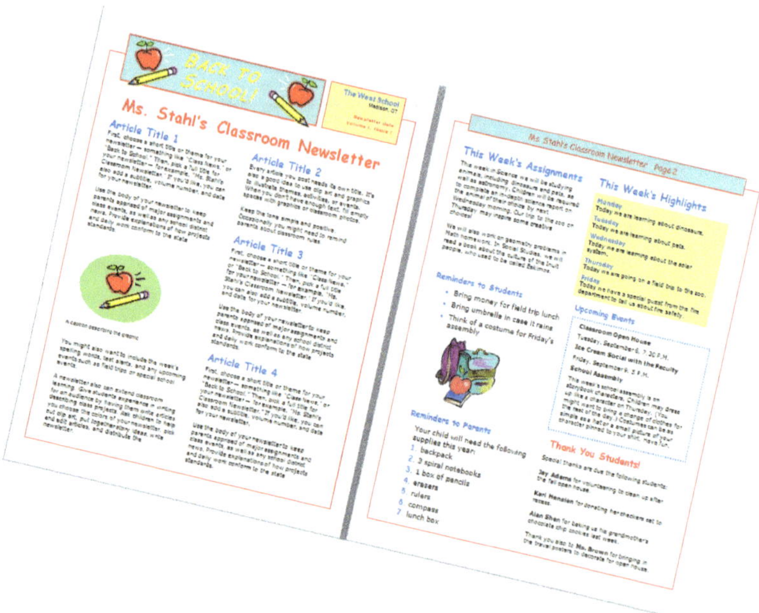

- What a newsletter is
- What a template is
- How to use text boxes in Word
- How to insert pictures in Word

What a newsletter is

A newsletter is a publication (periodical, pamphlet, etc.) that gets sent to its subscribers after a regular time interval (a week, a month, a year, etc.).

> *A newsletter is a publication (periodical, pamphlet, etc.) that gets passed out to its subscribers after a regular time interval (a week, a month, a year, etc.).*

Many people use newsletters to keep people informed of news and events in schools, families or clubs.

We will make a newsletter today to tell some of the stories happening in your world: either in your family, club or your school. It's your choice!

What a template is

A template is a pre-formatted document. It's easy to use because everything you need is already in place for you: words, pictures, page numbers, etc. This helps you know where everything belongs on the pages.

> *A template is a pre-formatted document.*

DO NOT DELETE the words and pictures already on the pages – they are there to help you. You need to carefully replace these "place holders" with the words and pictures that YOU want in your newsletter.

To replace text placeholders: Click once on the words and just start typing.

To replace pictures placeholders: Right-click on the picture, choose **Change Picture**.

Let's get started!

Step-By-Step

Follow the steps below to write a newsletter for your family or school using Microsoft Publisher.

1) <u>Open Microsoft Publisher 2019:</u>
   a) In Windows 10, click the **Start button** **OR in the** Search box type **Publisher 2019**
   b) Click **Publisher 2019**

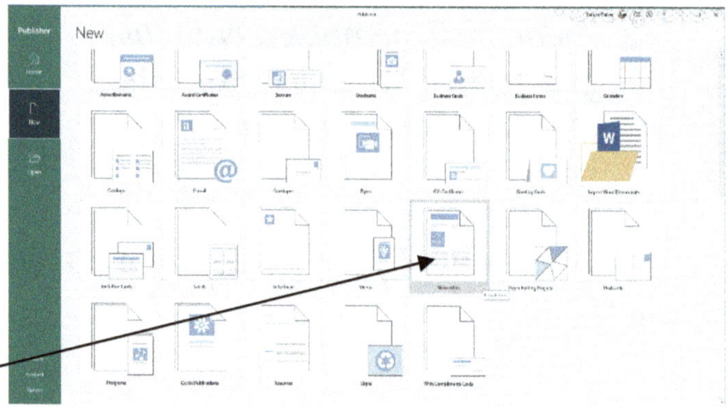

2) <u>Choose your template:</u>
   a) Click **BUILT-IN**
   b) Click once on **Newsletters**
   c) In the **Installed Templates** section, scroll down and look through the available templates
   d) Click ONCE on the **Newsletters** style that you want (I chose **School**)
3) <u>In the right pane, **Customize** the newsletter the way you want it:</u>
   a) <u>Change the Color scheme</u>
      i) Click **Color Scheme** on right side (some templates are not changed by this option)
      ii) Click a color scheme you like. Try as many as you like, only the last choice stays.
   b) <u>Change the Font scheme</u>
      i) Click **Font Scheme** on right side
      ii) Click a font scheme you like. Try as many as you like, only the last choice stays.
   c) <u>Under the Options section:</u>
      i) Under the **Page Size** section, click the arrow

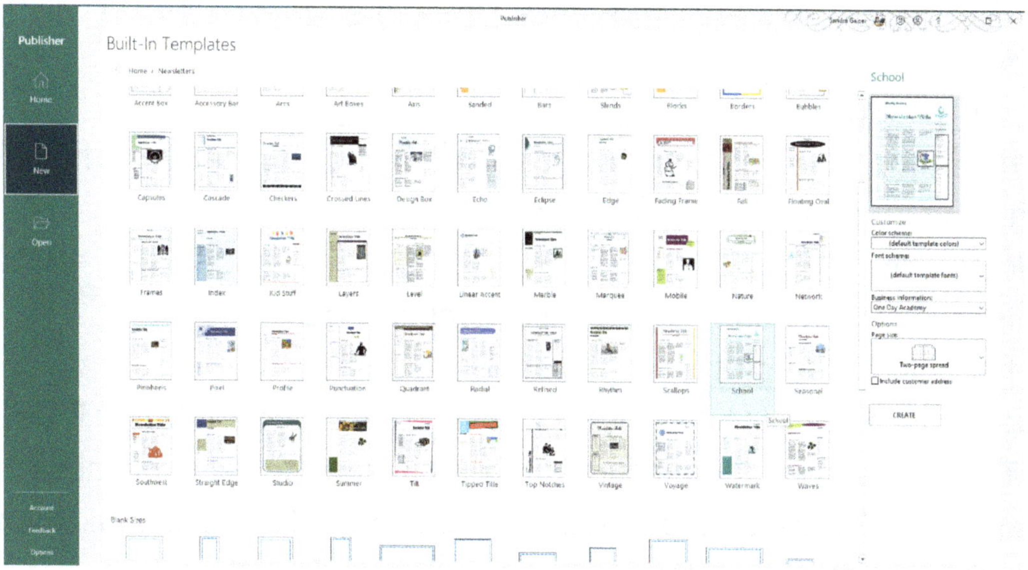

(1) Choose **One-Page spread** if you want a short newsletter and do not need the inside pages to be a mirror image of each other.

(2) Choose **Two-page spread** if you want a long newsletter and want the inside pages to mirror each other like a book.

ii) Check **Include customer address** if you plan to mail your newsletter.

d) Click **Create** when you're done

4) <u>Now let's type in the newsletter & story titles:</u>

a) Click inside the **Newsletter Title** box.

b) All the text is automatically selected in that text box.

c) Now, just start typing in your title (you don't have to press delete or backspace first).

Any text that is highlighted (or selected) will BE REPLACED with the next key you hit.

   d) Continue in this way until you have filled in all the titles for all the stories in your newsletter.

5) <u>Delete any extra pages you have and don't need:</u>
   a) In the **Pages** task pane, on the left side of the screen, right-click on each page that you **DO NOT WANT**.
   b) Click **Delete**
   c) Publisher will ask you if you are sure, click **YES**

6) <u>Now let's change the pictures:</u>
   a) Click on the first picture that you want to change – DO NOT DELETE IT. This will select the picture and its caption below it because these 2 items are **Grouped** (stuck together so they stay together when moved).
   b) Click one more time on the picture you want to change.
   c) Right-click the photo box with the arrow.

   d) Click **Change Picture**.
   e) Go to the folder where your picture is that you want to use. You can use online pictures or pictures you have on your computer or flash drive.
   f) Insert the picture.
   g) The picture will automatically fit into the box it was in.
   h) Change the picture caption below it by clicking in the box and typing the caption for your picture.

> **NOTE: If you want to resize the photo in a story, resize the placeholder BEFORE you change the picture. That way it won't get squished.**

   i) Continue in this way until you have filled in all the pictures for all the stories in your newsletter.

7) Now let's type in the stories:
   a) Click inside the first text box.
   b) Start typing your story.
   c) Make sure it fits in the area given to that story:
      i) You can Increase or Decrease your Font Size as needed: Press **CTRL-A** to select all the text in the story.

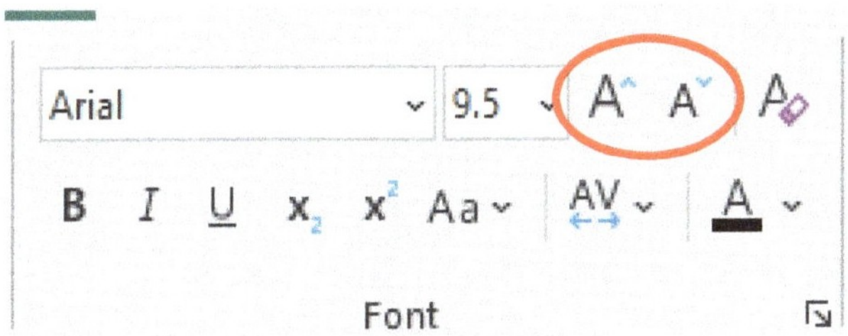

      ii) Click the **Increase Font Size** or **Decrease Font Size** buttons (on the **Home** tab, in the **Font** group) until the story fits in all the boxes.

The text boxes are connected or linked to each other so that when you run out of room in one box, it will continue typing in the next box.

   d) Continue in this way until you have filled in all the stories in your newsletter.

8) When you have finished, print the word document:
   a) Click **File**
   b) Click **Print**
   c) Click **Print**

9) To save the file:
   a) Click **File**
   b) Click **Save As**
   c) Type in Your name and project name (example: Nick's newsletter).
   d) Click **Save** button

Lesson 31 Practice

Day 1

1. **Follow the steps to make another newsletter.**
2. **Share it with a friend!**

Lesson Review:

1. What is a newsletter?

____

2. Why would text boxes be linked to each other?

____

3. What can you do to take up space if you run out of words to write?

____

Planning for our next lesson:

1. **What date is Mother's Day on this year?**

____

2. **What date is Father's Day on this year?**

____

Lesson

32

32-Mother & Father's Day Cards in Publisher

A nice way to remind any mother or father of how special they are!

About Our Project

We are going to use Microsoft Publisher to make a Mother's & Father's Day cards. Mother's Day is the 2nd Sunday each May, and Father's Day is the 3rd Sunday every June. Choose someone for which to make the cards: grandparents, aunts, uncles, or parents. Now, let's make some greeting cards!

What you will learn

- Review how to use a greeting card template
- Review how to change the layout of a greeting card
- Review how to change the color scheme
- Review how to change the font scheme

A Greeting Card

As you learned, Microsoft Publisher can make all kinds of greeting cards quickly. Since many templates are included for holidays and special occasions, I hope you have been making your own personalized cards for birthdays, anniversaries and other special occasions throughout this year! Remember, you can use the cards the way they are or **change any part of them** including the words, colors, pictures and styles.

Step-By-Step

Follow the steps below to create 2 Greeting Cards in Publisher.

1) Open Microsoft Publisher 2019:
   - a) In Windows 10, click the **Start button** **OR in the** Search box type **Publisher 2019**
   - b) Click **Publisher 2019**
   - c) Open a pre-designed Greeting Card:
   - d) Click **BUILT-IN**
   - e) Click on **Greeting Cards**
   - f) In the **Holidays** section, click on the **All Holidays** yellow folder
   - g) Scroll down the **Mother's Day & Father's Day** sections
   - h) Click ONCE on the card style that you want
2) In the right pane, **Customize** the card the way you want it:
   - a) Change the Color scheme
     - i) Click **Color Scheme** on right side
     - ii) Click a color scheme you like. Try as many as you like, only the last choice stays.
   - b) Change the Font scheme
     - i) Click **Font Scheme** on right side

ii) Click a font scheme you like. Try as many as you like, only the last choice stays.

c) Change the Page Size of the Card:

i) Choose **Quarter-fold** (prints on one side of paper) or **Half-fold** (prints on both sides of paper)

d) Change the Layout of the Card:

i) Choose one of 26 different layouts under **Layout** (lower right corner), click the little arrow

ii) Try different **Layouts** until you find the right one

e) Click **Create** when you're done

To change sides of the card, click in the Pages task pane on the left side of the window.

3) Customize the greeting card the way you want it:

a) Change the verse options

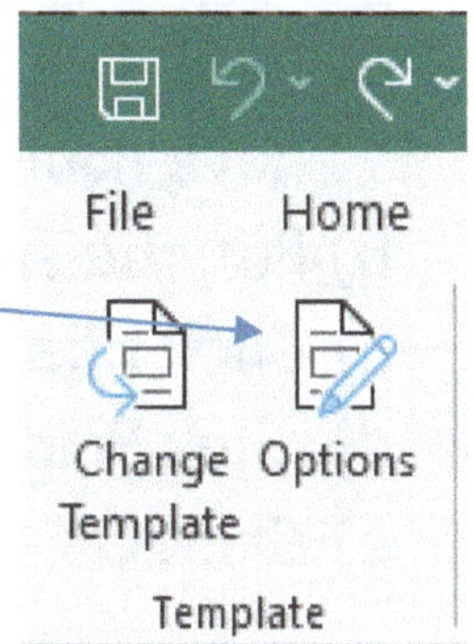

i) Click the **Page Design** tab on the **Ribbon**

ii) In the **Template** group, click the **Options** button with a pencil on it

iii) Click on the **Available Messages** on left side to see what they say on the right side of the window

iv) Click **OK** when you have chosen the one you want

OR You can type and change the words on all 4 sides of the card

b) Change the color scheme

i) On the **Ribbon**, click the **Page Design** tab

ii) Hover your mouse over the color schemes you like

iii) Click on the colors you like. Try as many as you like, only the last choice stays.

c) Change the font scheme
   i) On the **Ribbon**, click the **Page Design** tab
   ii) Click **Fonts**
   iii) Hover your mouse over the font schemes you like
   iv) Click a font scheme you like. Try as many as you like, only the last choice stays.
d) Insert Online or your own Pictures
   i) Click **Insert**
   ii) Click **Online Pictures** (for online images)
   iii) OR **Pictures** to find pictures on your own computer or USB drive
   iv) or **From File** (to use a photo you have taken)

4) When you have finished, print the card:
   a) These print best on greeting card paper or card stock, but if you have none, paper will work, too.
   b) Put the special paper in the printer, if you have some.
   c) Click **File**
   d) Click **Print**
   e) Click **OK**

If it's a Half-Fold card, don't forget to print the other side!!

   f) Fold your card
5) To save the file:
   a) Click **File**
   b) Click **Save As**
   c) Type in Your name and project name (example: Nick's Greeting card)
   d) Click **Save** button.
6) Now, go back to Step #1 and make the other card.

Lesson 32 Practice

Day 1

1. **Follow the steps to make another greeting card.**
2. **Print it out.**
3. **Give it!**

Lesson Review:

1. How do you insert a picture into a card?

____

2. Which is bigger: a half-fold card or a quarter-fold card?

____

3. How do you change the verse (or words) in a greeting card?

____

Planning for our next lesson:

1. **What books have you read this year?**

   ____

   ____

2. **What books do you plan to read this summer?**

   ____

   ____

3. **Have you ever participated in a summer reading program?**
   Yes No

Lesson

33

33-A Summer Reading Form in Excel

A nice form to keep track of all the wonderful summer reading you will do!

About Our Project

We are going to make a form in Excel to write down information about all the books we read this summer. It will show the title of the book, the minutes or chapters that were read. This is great to use to enter all those summer reading programs at your local libraries & bookstores!

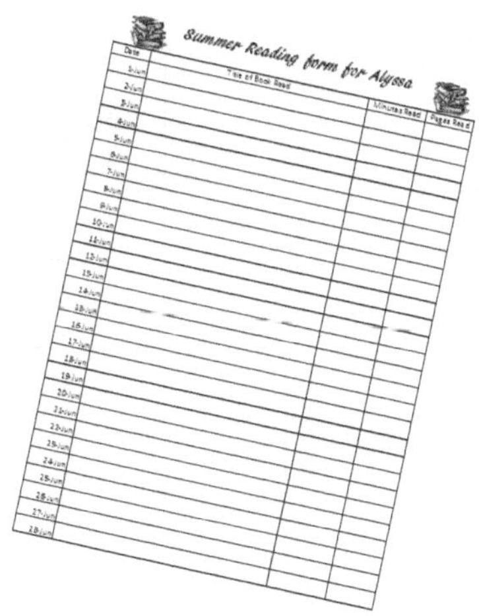

What you will learn

- What a summer reading form is
- Review what Excel is
- Review what a spreadsheet is
- Review how to add & delete text in Excel
- Review how to widen columns and rows
- Review how to add borders to cells
- Wrap & align text

What is a summer reading form?

A summer reading from is used to keep track of what books you read, how many chapters or pages and/or how many minutes or hours you have read. At the end, you can total it up and see just how much you read over the summer.

Summer Reading form for Alyssa

Date	Title of Book Read	Minutes Read	Pages Read
1-Jun			
2-Jun			
3-Jun			
4-Jun			
5-Jun			
6-Jun			
7-Jun			
8-Jun			
9-Jun			
10-Jun			
11-Jun			
12-Jun			
13-Jun			
14-Jun			
15-Jun			
16-Jun			
17-Jun			
18-Jun			
19-Jun			
20-Jun			
21-Jun			
22-Jun			
23-Jun			
24-Jun			
25-Jun			
26-Jun			
27-Jun			
28-Jun			

Review: What is Excel?

Excel is a spreadsheet program. A spreadsheet is a document with only rows and columns, like a big table in Word. It is a good way to work with information that is best stored in rows and columns, like:

- Names and addresses
- A budget that shows money coming in like paychecks and money going out as expenses
- Forms that you fill out
- Numbers that you need to add, subtract, multiply, divide or other math functions

Spreadsheets are **big**. In Microsoft Office 2019, one sheet can hold 16,384 columns and 1,048,576 rows. When you multiply those two, you find how many cells (little boxes of information) in one spreadsheet:

16,384 columns x 1,048,576 rows = 17,179,869,184 cells per worksheet

Wow! That's over 17 million cells!

And that's only in 1 worksheet. Each file is called a **workbook** and can hold more than one worksheet. How many worksheets in one Excel Workbook? Well, as many as your computer's memory can hold all at once. But, in the 2003 version, you could have 255 sheets. Imagine:

17,179,869,184 cells per worksheet x 255 =

4,380,866,641,920 cells in 1 workbook

Over 4 billion cells of information in 1 Excel workbook file! That is a lot of information.

To go to the last row, press CTRL-🡻
To go to the last column, press CTRL-🡺

To add text in Excel:

Simply click on a cell and type!

To delete text in Excel:

Simply click on a cell and press the Delete key!

To align text in Excel:

Simply select the cells you want to align the text in and click one of the **Alignment** buttons on the **Ribbon**, on the Home tab, in the **Alignment** group.

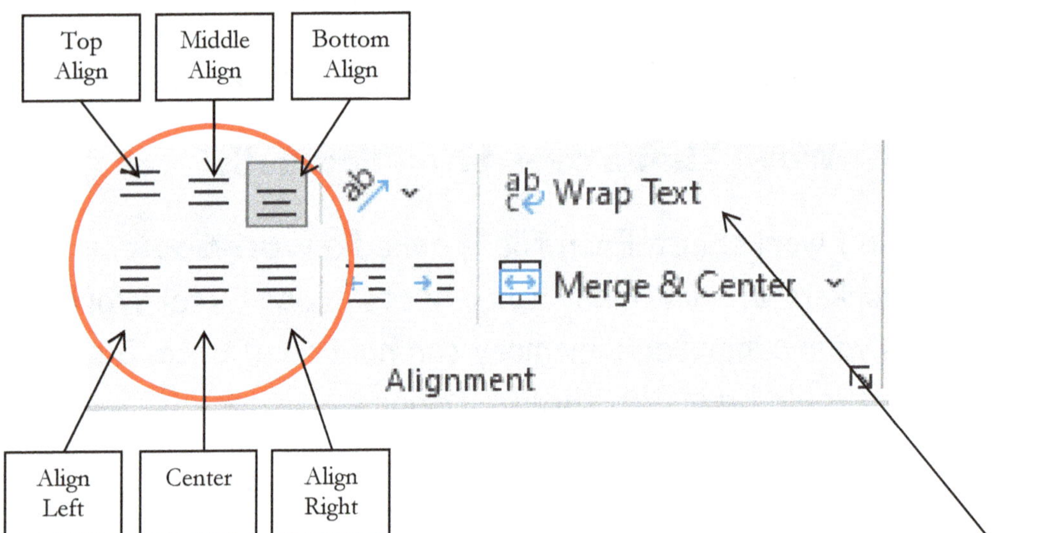

To wrap text in Excel:

Simply select the cells where you want the text to wrap and click the **Wrap Text** button on the **Ribbon**, on the Home tab, in the **Alignment** group.

To widen columns and rows:

Simply hover your mouse between any 2 columns or rows until you get a black, 2-headed arrow, then click and drag, or double-click to resize automatically.

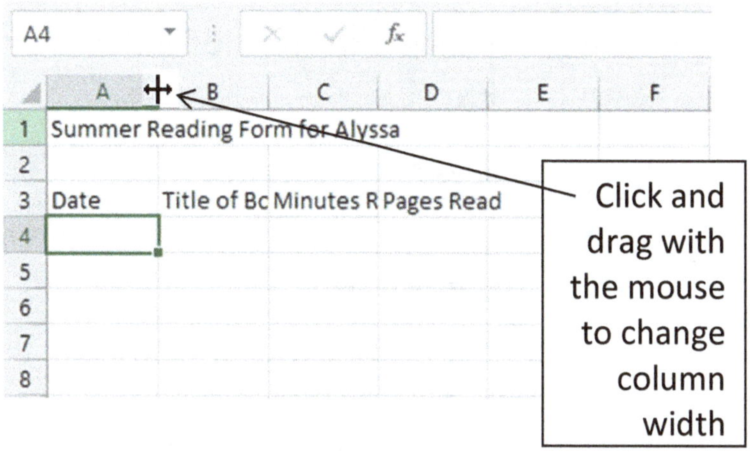

To add borders to cells (because be default they aren't any):

Simply select all the cells you want borders on, and click the borders button on the Ribbon in the Paragraph group on the Home tab.

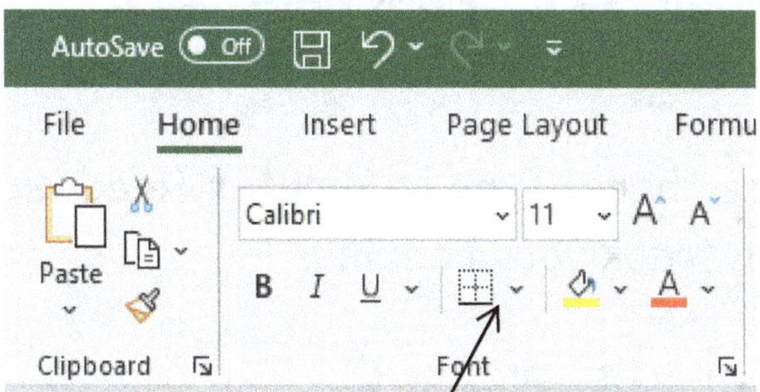

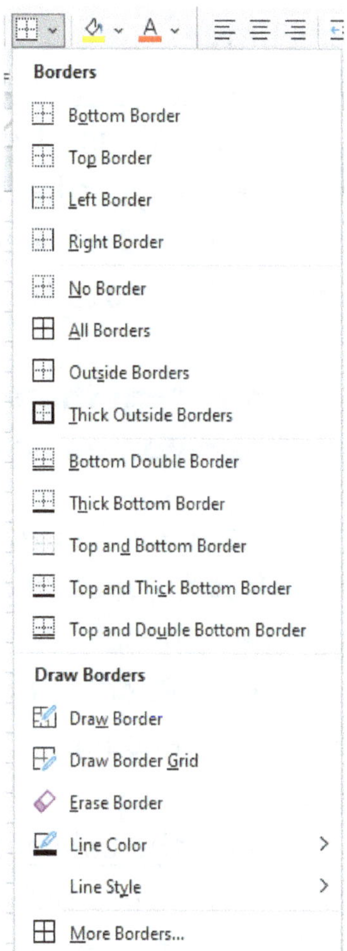

Click the tiny arrow to the right for choices of borders:

Step-By-Step

Follow the steps below to create a Summer Reading Form in Excel.

1) Open Microsoft Excel 2019:
   a) In Windows 10, click the **Start button** **OR in the** Search box type **Excel 2019**
   b) Click **Excel 2019**
2) Click **Blank workbook**
3) Title the Summer Reading form:
   a) In cell A1 and type **Summer Reading Form for (your name)**
   b) Press **Enter**
4) Now let's enter the column headings:
   a) Click on cell A3 and type **Date**
   b) Press **TAB** on your keyboard to move to cell B3
   c) Type **Title of Book Read**
   d) Press **TAB** to move to cell C3.

Don't worry that there is text already in C3 right now. We'll widen the columns next.

   e) Type right over the words that are there. Type in **Minutes Read or Hours Read**, depending on how you track your reading.
   f) Press **TAB** to move to cell D3
   g) Type **Pages Read** or **Chapters Read**, depending on how you want to track your reading.
   h) Press **Enter**
5) Now, to widen the columns:
   a) Hover your mouse between the column heading letters **B** and **C**. You should see a two-headed black arrow.

b) When you do, double-click your mouse. The column will resize to the perfect width.

c) But we want the column wider to hand-write in long book titles, so hover your mouse between the column heading letters **B** and **C** again and click and hold the mouse button down and drag it to the right as far as you need. **(350 pixels)** wide should be perfect.

Don't widen columns C or D right now – we'll wrap the text instead.

6) <u>Let's center, wrap & align the column headings:</u>
   a) Click right on the row number 3 to select the whole row.
   b) Click the **Center** button on the **Ribbon** in the **Alignment** group.
   c) Now, click on **Wrap Text**, also in the **Alignment** group. Now you can read the words nicely.
   d) Now, click on **Middle Align**, also in the **Alignment** group above the **Center** button. Now all text is well-centered, vertically & horizontally.

7) <u>Now, to enter the dates:</u>
   a) Click on cell A4 and type **June 1** and press **Enter**. It will change to 1-Jun. That's fine. That's the default date format in Excel.

Excel puts the day number first, before the month name so it can sort dated information easily.

b) Click on cell A4 again and put your mouse in the lower right corner. The mouse pointer should change to a little black plus sign (+).

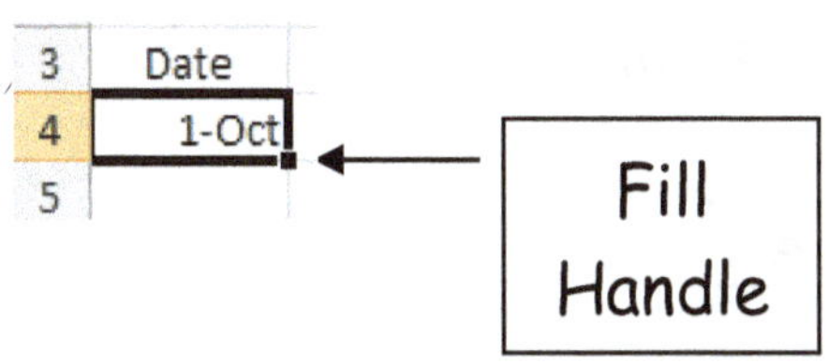

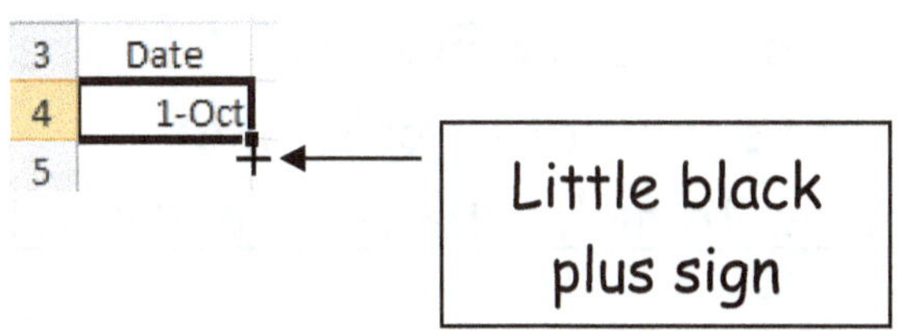

When you see that, click and hold your mouse button down and drag 75 rows until the date box says August 15. Then let go of the mouse. Now we have lines for every day this summer!

- c) Scroll back up to the top of the spreadsheet or press **CTRL-HOME** to get back to cell A1.

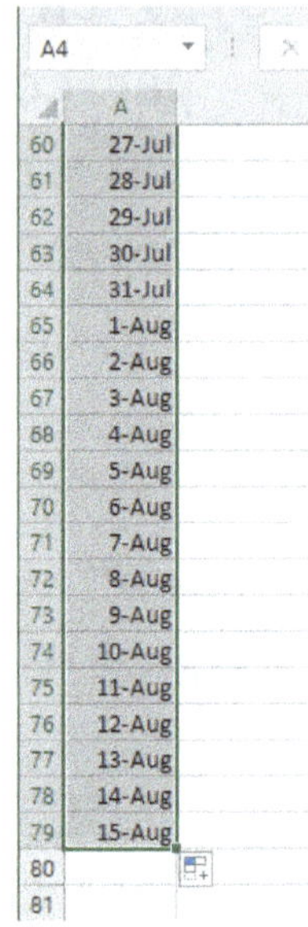

8) <u>Let's widen the rows now so you can write in them:</u>
   - a) Select all the rows by clicking on row number 4 and dragging down to last row with a date (row 79).
   - b) Hover you mouse between any 2 row numbers and click and drag until they are 30 pixels wide.
   - c) Scroll up to the top.
   - d) Click anywhere to deselect everything.

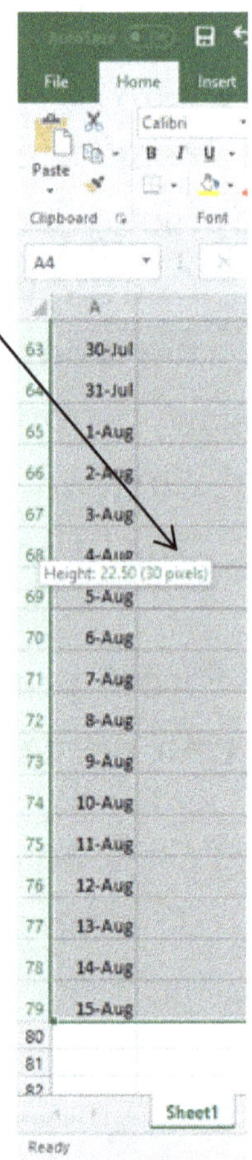

9) Now take a look in **Print Preview**:
   - a) Click **File**
   - b) Click **Print**

10) <u>What's missing? Lines! They are called **Borders** in Excel. Let's add them:</u>
   - a) To select all your rows and columns: Click on cell **A3**, holding down your mouse button, drag over to cell **D3** and continue downward till you reach the last row starting with 15-Aug (Cell **D79**). Let go of the mouse button.
   - b) On the **Ribbon**, in the **Font** group, look for the **Bottom Border button** (□). Click the tiny, black arrow next to the box.
   - c) Click on **All Borders**.
   - d) Now click on **File, Print** to preview the form again to see what it looks like.

11) <u>Now to make the title look a little nicer:</u>

a) Click on **A1** and drag over to **D1** to select the top row of the first page.
b) On the **Ribbon**, in the **Alignment Group**, click **Merge and Center**.
c) With it still selected, change the font style and size (22 is a good title size font).
d) Change the **Font Style & Color**, too - you know how to now!

12) **Insert** a tiny **Online Picture** of a book or the sun in the upper left and right corner.

13) <u>We have 3 pages, so we want the title row to repeat at the top of each page. Here's how:</u>
a) On the **Ribbon**, click the **Page Layout** tab.
b) Click the **Print Titles** button in the **Page Setup** group.

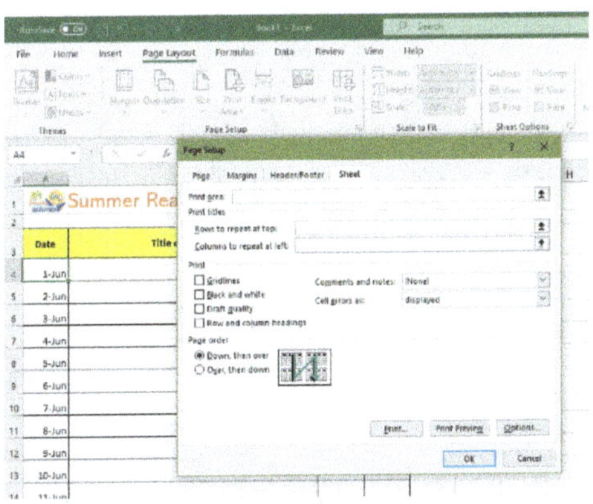

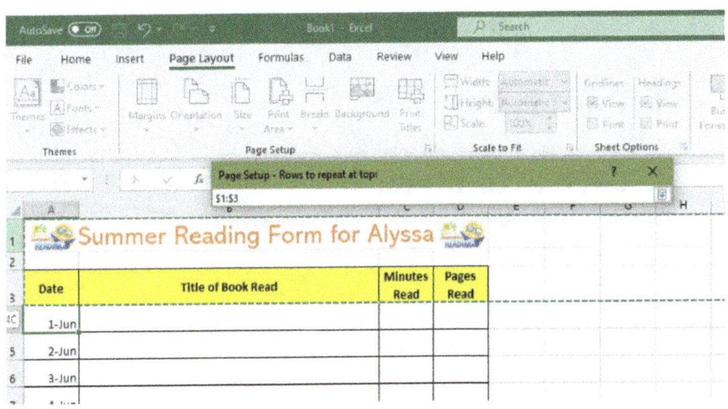

c) Click inside the **Rows to Repeat at Top** box.
d) Click on the row number 1, drag down to select rows 2 & 3 also.
e) Press **Enter**.
f) Click **OK**.

14) <u>When you have finished, print the form:</u>
a) Click **File**
b) Click **Print**
c) Click **Print**

15) <u>To save the file:</u>

a) Click **File**
b) Click **Save As**
c) Choose where you want the file to be saved
d) Type in Your name and project name (example: Nick's Summer Reading form).
e) Click **Save** button

Lesson 33 Practice

Day 1

1. Follow the steps to make another summer reading form for a sibling or a friend.

2. Print it out.

3. Give it to them.

Lesson Review:

1. Does Excel print out lines between all the cells by default?

____

2. How do you merge and center the cells to make a title look nicer?

____

3. How do you widen columns in Excel?

____

Lesson

34

34-Award Certificates in Publisher

A nice form to keep and remind you of all you leaned this year!

About Our Project

We are going to use Microsoft Publisher to make an Award Certificate for your completion of this class. It will include the name of this class, your name, and a place for your teacher to sign and date it. Congratulations!!

What you will learn

- What is an award certificate is
- How to use an award certificate template
- How to change text on an award certificate template
- How to change the color scheme on an award certificate template
- How to change the font scheme on an award certificate template

What is an award certificate?

An award certificate is a **special document** that is given to someone **to acknowledge an accomplishment** by them. In this case, this award certificate will mark **your successful completion** of this office applications course for kids! **Congratulations!**

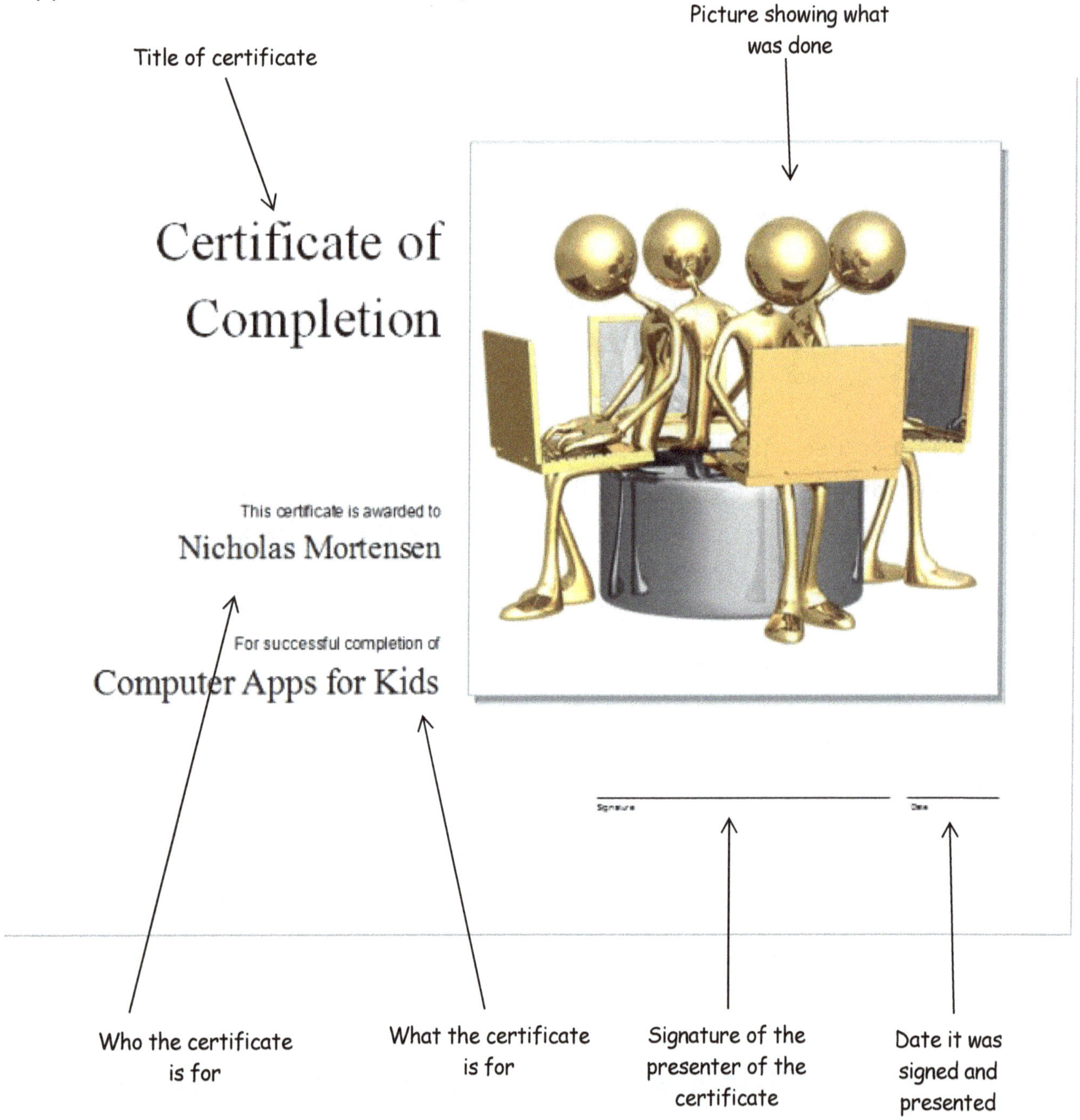

Step-By-Step

Follow the steps below to create an Award Certificate in Publisher for the completion of this class.

1) Open Microsoft Publisher 2019:
   a) In Windows 10, click the **Start button** **OR in the** Search box type **Publisher 2019**
   b) Click **Publisher 2019**
2) Choose your award certificate template:
   a) Click **BUILT-IN**
   b) Click once on **Award Certificates**
   c) Click ONCE on the style you like (don't double-click or you will go right into the publication before you can choose your options)
3) In the right pane, Customize the certificate the way you want it:
   a) Change the Color scheme
      i) Click **Color Scheme** on right side
      ii) Click a color scheme you like. Try as many as you like, only the last choice stays.
   b) Change the Font scheme
      i) Click **Font Scheme** on right side
      ii) Click a font scheme you like. Try as many as you like, only the last choice stays.
4) Click **Create**

Remember: You can change any part of a template from colors to fonts to text and placement of objects.

5) Change the certificate information:
   a) Click in the title and change it to **Certificate of Completion**
   b) Change **"Name of Recipient"** to your name

- c) Change "**In recognition for valuable contributions to**" to say "**For successful completion of**"
- d) Change "**Business Name**" to "**Office Apps for Kids**"
- e) If your award certificate template doesn't have a business name text box, then draw a text box:
  - i) Click the **Insert** tab on the **Ribbon**
  - ii) In the **Text** group, click **Draw Text Box**

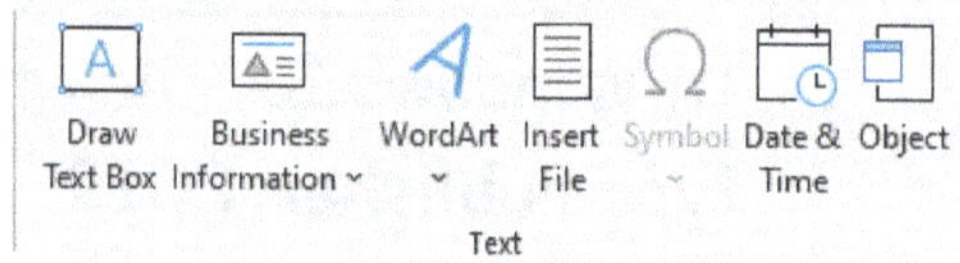

  - iii) Click under **the "For successful completion of"** box and drag to right and pull down.
  - iv) Type **"Office Apps for Kids"**

6) Change or add a large image of a laptop or computer:
   - a) If there is a large picture on your template that you chose, right-click it to select it and chose **Change Picture**
   - b) If there isn't already a large picture, click on the **Insert** tab on the **Ribbon** and click **Online Pictures** and search for a picture of a laptop
   - c) Click on the picture you like to add it to your certificate
7) Delete the extra signature line and date line and text boxes:
   - a) Click on each line & text box **edge** and press **Delete** on your keyboard
8) When you have finished, print the certificate:
   - a) Click **File**
   - b) Click **Print**
   - c) Click **Print**
9) To save the file:
   - a) Click **File**
   - b) Click **Save As**
   - **c)** Choose where you want to save your file
   - d) Type in Your name and project name (example: Nick's Certificate)
   - e) Click **Save** button
10) Have your teacher sign and date your certificate

Congratulations! You did a great job!

Lesson 34 Practice

Day 1

1. **Follow the steps and make another certificate in Publisher for someone in your family: Best Dad, Super Brother, Great Sister, and Awesome Mom!**
2. **Print it out.**
3. **Hand it to them and watch them smile!** ☺

Appendix A

Keyboard Shortcuts

CTRL-P	print
CTRL-Z	undo
CTRL-Y	redo (what you undid)
CTRL-X	cut
CTRL-C	copy
CTRL-V	paste
CTRL-B	bold

Appendix

B

Appendix B

Materials Needed to Teach This Book:

- A color printer
- Sticker printer paper
- Plain printer paper
- #10 envelopes
- Return address labels
- Card Stock
- Light T-Shirt transfer paper
- Regular-sized bags of original Skittles®, 1 per student
- Printer business card paper

Index

www.ingramcontent.com/pod-product-compliance
Lightning Source LLC
LaVergne TN
LVHW060031210926
848481LV00013B/3833